D0375271

ECOLOGICAL
GARDENING

Also by Marjorie Harris

How to Make a Garden
Botanica North America
The Canadian Gardener
Seasons of My Garden
Marjorie Harris' Favorite Garden Tips
Pocket Gardening
In the Garden
Favorite Annuals
Favorite Flowering Shrubs
Favorite Perennials
Favorite Shade Plants
The Canadian Gardener's Year
The Canadian Gardener

ECOLOGICAL GARDENING

Your safe path to
a healthy, beautiful garden

MARJORIE HARRIS

RANDOM HOUSE CANADA

Copyright © 1991, 1996, 2009 Marjorie Harris

All rights reserved under International and Pan-American Copyright
Conventions. No part of this book may be reproduced in any form
or by any electronic or mechanical means, including information
storage and retrieval systems, without permission in writing from the
publisher, except by a reviewer, who may quote brief passages in a
review. Originally published in 1996 by Random House Canada,
a division of Random House of Canada Limited, Toronto. Second
edition published in 1996. Third edition published in 2009.
Distributed by Random House of Canada.

www.randomhouse.ca

Random House Canada and colophon are trademarks

Library and Archives Canada Cataloguing in Publication
Harris, Marjorie
Ecological gardening / Marjorie Harris.

ISBN 978-0-307-35735-9

1. Organic gardening—Canada. 2. Garden ecology—Canada.
I. Title.
SB453.5.H37 2009   635'.04840971   C2008-906514X

This book is printed on paper that is ancient-forest friendly
(100% post-consumer recycled) and chlorine-free.

Design by Kelly Hill

Printed in the United States of America

10 9 8 7 6 5 4 3 2 1

For Auntie Marge
and all the other gardeners
who are serious about
our survival on this
beautiful planet

CONTENTS

CONTENTS

ACKNOWLEDGEMENTS

Thanks to Chris Harris who worked incredibly hard on the research for this edition; Dr. Laurence Packer of York University for close reading of the bug chapter; the wonderful writing of Bridget Stutchberry, Janet Benyus and Michael Pollan; Karen York, Sonia Day and Juliet Mannock who always make good suggestions on how to garden well. I'd also like to thank the design and editorial teams at Random House Canada—Kelly Hill, Erin Cooper, Amanda Lewis, Kylie Barker, Deirdre Molina, and especially Anne Collins for agreeing to bring my book back to life.

INTRODUCTION

Things have changed drastically since I first set out to research the first edition of this book in the late 1980s. We certainly knew that something strange was going on with the planet, but it was a time of "progress" as long as it came in a package or a pill. In those days, being an organic gardener seemed like a throwback to an ancient time, being an environmentalist (think tree-hugger) conjured up all sorts of ridicule and the idea of an ecological garden led to much head-scratching.

When I was interviewed on the subject, the first question was always: What on earth is an ecological garden? Explaining that an ecological garden is chemical-free was easy. Explaining that in order to create an ecological garden, you have to place the garden into the context of the ecosystem you find yourself in, involved a fair amount of additional head-scratching.

At the time I wrote: We know that the earth is one vast living, breathing system where everything relates to everything else. It fits together in a most delicate and exquisite way. The ecological garden is a metaphor for planet Earth—it is in itself an ecosystem that reflects this finely tuned, integrated whole. To be an ecological gardener means understanding both your place in this whole and how your garden functions within its own ecosystem; that is, the relationships between the soil, light, air, every insect and microbe and the plants you choose. It means being sensitive to the environment and less haphazard in your approach to the earth. The more exhausted the planet becomes, the more important it is to put back almost everything we take from it.

It's exciting to figure out the composition of soil, what plants need and how to put them together for a healthy, pest-resistant garden. On top of these benefits is the delight in watching how your own caretaking abilities expand. The slightest understanding of how all elements in nature mesh together adds to the pleasure of gardening.

In this book I've gathered together the relevant information you'll need to become an ecological gardener. Using the index, you can dip into sections as the need arises. Since I first wrote this book in 1990, some things have changed, but most of the basic information remains the same. As I said then, and I still firmly believe: We have a choice in the way we garden. We can continue to put a strain on the biosphere or we can try, in our own small ways, to return to a simpler form of gardening—a retrieving of wisdom. Many of the old ways are far more effective than any high-tech solutions. What's happened in the last few years is that we've discovered how much more complicated nature is than we had formerly divined. We simply have no idea how these systems work, or why. What we do know is that they are interdependent and that if you kill something off, be it a plant or an insect, something else is going to be affected.

There are some tough facts we have to face that can't be solved through better gardening techniques. Climate change, with its attendant wild weather patterns, is becoming more and more evident. We now know for certain that burning fossil fuels increases atmospheric gases, which lead, in turn, to increased temperatures. An increase of 1°C alters the architecture of some plants, which affects all other plants and animals dependent on them. The same rise in temperature is changing the structure of ice caps, leading to rising water levels. It's a domino effect—one thing leads to another.

James Hansen, a climate scientist at Columbia University, warned us back in 1988 and again in 2008 that even the slightest warming in temperature can push us to dangerous tipping points. In his article, "Global Warming Twenty Years Later", he wrote. "Global warming initiated sea ice melt, exposing darker ocean that absorbs more sunlight, melting more ice. As a result, without any additional greenhouse gases, the Arctic will soon be ice-free in the summer. . . . West Antarctic and Greenland ice sheets are vulnerable to even small additional warming. These two-mile-thick behemoths respond slowly at first, but if disintegration gets well underway, it will become unstoppable."

He talks about animals and plants becoming stressed by climate change; how polar and alpine species will be pushed off the planet; and the potential of ecosystem collapse. This has happened before, as Hansen points out, and recovery took hundreds of thousands of years. Climate change has accelerated in the past two decades. Desertification continues to expand in the southern U.S., Australia, southern Africa and the Mediterranean. Forest fires are becoming more intense. And the drying up of lakes will increase if carbon dioxide emissions are not halted.

We can't just buckle under all this depressing information and give up. What we have to remember as we try to make a difference in our own backyards is that it's not the planet we are saving. The planet will carry on inexorably without our species and probably turn back into Eden. It's us—our generation, our children and our grandchildren—who are at risk. What we have to save is our relationship to our only home. And we can start with the garden. The earth was a garden when we first began evolving, and we have a responsibility to return it to that state.

When I wrote the first edition of *Ecological Gardening*, I was nervous about climate change, but I thought sanity would prevail. That was then . . . . Now, even though politicians mouth the platitudes, they just don't get it. Our governments, big oil companies, coal lobbies, etc., would like to carry on as though nothing is wrong. We can't be fools and let them prevail.

Things can change. Look at the banning of plastic bags and the removal of phosphates from some detergents. Don't give up! Start with your own garden, then move on to the neighbourhood and then the country. You can change the way you live. If you go to the last chapter of this book, you'll find some of the smartest ways to make a difference that I've found over the past twenty years. What this book will show you is how to garden with Integrated Pest Management; how to know your enemy and its life cycles; how to rotate plants if you need to; and how to use pest-resistant plants and natural predators. Much of it is common sense.

Here are some of the basics to get you started on your ecological garden:

1. "Treat the soil, not the plant" is the litany of all organic gardeners. Improve your soil organically with compost and humus of your own making. It's the cheapest and best form of soil nutrition.

2. Get the hardiest plants—ones most resistant to disease— and concentrate on having a basic structure of native plants. These are the likeliest to survive the assault of our weather extremes.

3. Choose biodiversity for your garden. The more types of plants you have, the more good bugs you'll attract. They'll bump off the bad ones.

4. Think of your garden as an ecosystem in which every single thing (millions of microbes, thousands of insects and, you hope, hundreds of birds) is dependent on everything else. Anything that is likely to damage any aspect of this fragile balance should not be allowed to enter. Your garden is your sanctuary.

Gardens make a difference because they are refuges for millions of living creatures—especially for the pollinators on whom we depend. Whether you can see them or not, they add to the biodiversity of your street and your city.

1

SOIL

The Real Dirt

I was an organic gardener long before I knew what the term meant. When I started gardening decades ago, labels on fertilizer packages with 10–10–10 or 2–10–whatever baffled me. These products all seemed to be manufactured by the same big chemical companies that I was, no doubt, boycotting because of their involvement in the Vietnam War. Since I was composting out of habit and the garden seemed healthy enough, I didn't bother with synthetic fertilizers. Through laziness I was doing exactly what I should have been doing— ecological gardening by default.

The most important philosophical gardening question to ask yourself is this: What is the nature of soil? Think for a moment about how we even acquired this miraculous substance. Over millions of years, massive upheavals around the world exposed huge rocks, then glacial movements scoured them clean. In the retreat of the great ice sheets, moraines, boulders and clay were left behind. They became deposits of gravel and sand as they were pounded away by wind and rain. Over the eons, through the action of bacteria, fungi, lichens, insects and eventually earthworms, thin layers of soil emerged.

In fact, the earth you stand on in your garden seethes with life. Imagine big animals devouring little animals, think of ancient migrations and the drama of birth and death all going on in a dark world that requires oxygen and water to survive. Sounds a lot like what happens on top of the soil, doesn't it? Though we are very concerned about the quality of our air, we seldom think about this other part of the biosphere.

Half the soil consists of solid material, mostly mineral particles, and half consists of the spaces between this material; and half of these, in turn, are filled with water that occurs as a film around the particles. All these microscopic bits and pieces are so vital that without them we would be doomed.

What's taking place in this subterranean world is a cycle of death and decomposition, as one kind of organism becomes food for others. Eventually these death throes supply all the nutrients needed by plants. The ultimate in recycling. Every plant you add has a function within this community: some fix nitrogen in the soil, some are deep-rooted, diving downwards for water, while others with shallow roots take advantage of limited rain.

The most devastating part of all this is that we are ill-informed about these relationships and even the cleverest of scientists doesn't know the whole story. Most of us seldom think about soil at all. Life is churning away beneath our feet and yet every move we make serves to kill it off. Our prairies once had the most fertile soil in the world, an extraordinary humus created over thousands of years. We've managed to deplete it in a century with one-crop farming (monoculture), ripping out the native grasses (polyculture) that held it in place, leaving it exposed to the elements, and allowing humongous machinery to drive over and compact it. All this activity conspires to destroy the life below the surface. Add the assault of chemical fertilizers almost non-stop for forty years, plus pollution, fires and floods and you'll begin to understand what's happening to this fragile ecosystem.

The microscopic animals of the soil live a full life if they are allowed to. They browse, swim, travel, have profligate sex lives, procreate and die, providing food for the big guys—arthropods and earthworms. The symbiosis among these animals is highly structured. What happens when we interfere chemically with all this activity is that we slowly poison the soil by killing off mites, bacteria, fungi and, even worse, earthworms. The remaining species multiply. This throws off the balance entirely as the level of chemicals steadily increases until the soil becomes toxic to plants, animals and people.

What keeps the soil healthy are all these organisms in the perpetual process of decomposition. Dying matter breaks down into humus and, through this, releases nutrients for plants. When we put the soil in jeopardy, our very survival is in question.

Dr. Stuart B. Hill, professor of entimology and soil guru, says that rather than killing off bacteria and fungi, we should be investigating and developing management strategies for their productive potential.

"Such strategies," he maintains, "are likely to save money, energy, and avoid damage to the support environment and to human and livestock health. This contrasts with our current approach, which involves the removal of several dozen minerals at harvest time followed by the replacement of only a few of them as chemical fertilizers" (*Agricultural Chemicals and the Soil* [1977]).

Bioagriculturists consider pests and diseases to be symptoms of poor soil management. Pesticides, antibiotics and drugs

have generally been regarded as "magic bullets" that can eliminate problems. "The real situation," Dr. Hill says, "is that we do
not suffer from pests because of a deficiency of pesticide in
the environment just as we do not get a headache because of
a deficiency of aspirin in the blood." Keep that line in mind
when you get into an argument with a chemical pusher.

This dependency on chemicals *is* much like an addiction.
The more you use, the more you need merely to survive. But
the depletion of soil expands exponentially, and what little
short-term gain there is for the private person will eventually
become a huge costly public burden as we all try to recover
the health of our soil.

The soil has amazing strategies of its own for dealing with
harmful things. For instance, there are nematodes that are
dreadful killers. They get into the roots of plants and suck
them dry. To counter this, there are fungi that strangle the
bad nematodes. Most other nematodes are helpful to the soil;
some kill off plant pests.

To give you an idea of just how complex all of this is, consider that there may be a hundred thousand protozoa in the
water that surrounds a few particles of soil. The millions of
bacteria in each gram of soil are crucial to decomposition. To
aid the process, there's the activity of earthworms.

EARTHWORMS

Aristotle referred to earthworms as the intestines of the earth
and Darwin called them nature's ploughmen. Earthworms,
Darwin calculated, could move 7.5 to 18 tonnes of soil per
acre (0.4 ha) annually.

North American earthworms are thought to have been
pretty much done in by the last ice age. One of the things
Europeans did when they came to this continent was to bring

earthworms with them. There are now twenty-three recorded species in Canada, including a couple of native ones. Earthworms eat up fallen leaves and start the whole decomposition process, though they won't work on fresh beech or oak leaves with the same efficiency as on other leaves. They gobble up organic matter and leave behind castings filled with calcium, potassium and phosphorus; they stir up the soil and bring nutritional material closer to the surface and more accessible to plants; and they aerate the soil through burrows that bring oxygen to the bacteria that need it to survive. Their burrows also provide channels for roots and increase the ability of water to move through the soil.

Worms aid in creating the all-important humus. They hate anything that messes with soil life—especially synthetic fertilizers. So we should be aware of worms' value. In each square yard (metre) of healthy soil, there will be about 300 earthworms. In anything but really acidic soil, if you haven't got a lot of wormy activity, you've got a problem.

KNOW YOUR SOIL

No doubt there is a platonic form that contains the perfect soil: dark loam containing enough balanced humus to hold just the right amount of rain but with excellent drainage. It's out there somewhere, but the soil most of us are usually presented with has something wrong with it: too heavy, too sandy, too much clay and always, always, the possibility of past over-cultivation. This can happen in a few seasons if nothing organic is put back into the soil. What your soil probably needs is some form of conditioning.

Fertile soil is the result of a cumulative process of continuous improvement. Two things are required: humus and finely ground rock particles. The latter make up the mineral portion of the soil. But it is the humus or organic matter that is most important. Dr. Hill refers to the humus-creation process as a primitive form of farming that's been going on for 400 million years. What keeps the farm thriving is the decomposition of organic matter.

Organic matter is comprised of living matter, such as leaves, in the process of decay. To break down, leaves need many different fungi, each with a special function, to attack them. Then there are mites and other arthropods that come next. If you destroy any of these with pesticides, you can upset the balance needed for proper decomposition. Since most of these creatures are beneficial, it seems unnecessary to go on a chemical rampage for the few that might be malevolent. You might also destroy their natural predators, thus reducing any short-term good that the chemicals might provide.

Some organisms, such as mycorrhizal fungi, perform Herculean tasks in the soil. They not only improve plant health, they also help plants absorb phosphorus, so essential to growth, and assimilate trace elements, which assist plants in withstanding the stress of drought. Experiments in how to use these fungi as an inoculum are now under way. And what do they need in order to prosper? Aerated soil with lots of organic matter. But they won't co-operate if pesticides and herbicides have been used.

FEED THE SOIL

The more intimate you are with your soil, the better handle you'll have on dealing with any problems that arise. To feed the soil, you need to know what the menu should be.

THE STRUCTURE OF SOIL Soil comes in layers. Depending on how great your soil is, each layer will be from a few inches (centimetres) to a few feet (metres) thick. Arising from the bedrock of the earth, soil is like a thin skin on its surface. It takes about 500 years to create 1 inch (2.5 centimetres) of soil through weathering.

The texture of soil depends on the sand, clay and silt content. The ideal loam is 25 percent water and 25 percent air, with the balance made up of organic matter—all the animals and tiny organisms that live there plus minerals. In this same ideal soil, micro-organisms release 3 pounds (1.3 kilograms) of nitrogen a year, which is about the equivalent of a 50-pound (23-kilogram) bag of 6–10–4 commercial fertilizer. All of the nitrogen and sulphur, and one-third of the phosphorus and other nutrients are supplied by organic matter.

Humus: The top layer of organic matter, decayed and in the process of decaying, is humus. It helps the soil absorb water, provides air spaces critical to plant development and is filled with the nutrients plants need for survival.

Topsoil: This is where the life of your soil is found. Earthworms, bacteria and a multitude of other animal organisms live here. It contains minerals and organic matter ranging from 49 percent to 1 percent, depending on the location. The depth could be from a fraction of an inch (a few millimetres) to 18 inches (45 centimetres) or more.

Subsoil: There are fewer nutrients at this level. The material here is pulverized and there's no humus. But soil conditioning can help improve a shallow subsoil.

Hardpan: This is self-descriptive. Clay and silt make it almost impermeable. At this level there is little or no drainage. The closer to the surface you find hardpan, the more shallow-rooted the plants will be.

Bedrock: There is no soil below this level.

TYPES OF SOIL To evaluate your soil, dig out a chunk of earth approximately 12 inches (30 centimetres) deep. Now pull a fistful from the centre of the batch. Moisten it slightly and then squeeze it in your hand to figure out what type of soil you have.

Heavy: If the moistened soil holds the shape of your hand, you've got heavy—or clay—soil. Clay has very few spaces between the tiny particles. That means it has poor drainage and is slow to warm up in the spring. It needs to be lightened up with organic matter, such as humus or compost, plus sand, for improved drainage.

Perfect: The best soil, loam, is 40 percent sand, 40 percent silt, 20 percent clay. It's great stuff, perfectly balanced. When you squeeze it, it makes a ball that falls apart easily. It drains readily, which is what, ideally, you are aiming for. Once you have loam, keep adding compost or humus to keep it up to scratch.

Light: Mainly sandy, light soil won't hold together in your fist. It's very gritty stuff with large particles that let water drain away far too quickly. This kind of soil needs an underlying level of humus or organic matter such as well-rotted leaves.

Mixed: Silty loam feels smooth and holds its shape. Sandy loam is gritty and forms a ball. If you have a soggy mess of mucky peat soil that just sort of plops in the hand, it needs serious amending.

SOIL TESTING If you're unsure whether you have acid or alkaline soil, have it tested at a garden centre, agricultural station or soil laboratory. There are also kits available that are relatively efficient.

To prepare a soil test, dig a sample from every 100 square feet (9 square metres) to a depth of 6 to 12 inches (15 to 30 centimetres). Mix the sample in a bucket and send about a pint (1/2 litre) of this mix to be tested. If you describe what you want to plant, the soil can be tested for that purpose. You will be given the nutrient content, pH and a description of texture. On the pH scale of 0 to 14, acid soil is below 7, neutral soil is 7, and alkaline soil is above 7. Most plants—and soil organisms—like a pH between 6.5 and 7.

ACID SOIL—BELOW 7.0 pH A fast way to figure out if you have acid soil is to take a small amount and add a bit of vinegar. If the vinegar sizzles, you've got alkaline soil. If not, that means there's acid in it and the vinegar (itself an acid) won't react with it. Weeds will also let you know if you have acid soil: meadow foxtails, daisies, mouse-ear hawkweed, corn marigold or corn chrysanthemum, corn spurry, sheep sorrel, sow thistle, coltsfoot, nettles and masses of Johnny-jump-ups all indicate acid soil.

FOR PLANTS NEEDING ACID SOIL If you don't have acid soil but want to grow acid-loving plants such as rhododendrons, azaleas and heaths, which like a pH of 4.5 to 6.0, try the following:
- Dig out a bed 18 inches (45 centimetres) deep and fill with a mixture of sharp sand and garden loam to 3 parts coir, or sawdust from pines or oak. Add 5 pounds (2 kilograms) of sulphur per 100 square feet (9 square metres).
- Once the acid-loving plant is in place, add 2 teaspoons (10 grams) of powdered sulphur every square foot (.09 square metre).
- To acidify the soil in a small area, you can also try adding vinegar and coffee grounds a little bit at a time.

Maintenance:
- Don't use peat moss. Though over time it will acidify the soil, it's a non-renewable resource and is sterile. If

you insist on peat moss, soak it with hot water and let it sit; this will help it to add moisture-retention qualities to the soil. Dig it in and allow the bed to winter over before planting.

* Don't use bone meal or wood ashes—both contain lime and will reduce the acidity of the soil.
* Check out the rainwater. In many cities, rain is becoming increasingly acidic due to pollution. Collect rainwater in drums and use it to water acid-loving plants.
* Mulch with leaf mould from oaks and pines.

To Reduce Soil Acidity:
* Lime will reduce acidity. Dolomitic limestone contains magnesium and calcium, thus fertilizing the soil at the same time. It is the recommended form. Apply in the fall after the ground is dug or ploughed, to give it a chance to break down—which it does very slowly.
* Wood ashes are about 20 to 50 percent calcium carbonate and thus will act quickly to reduce acidity. They are high in phosphorus. The best time to apply is late winter or early spring, but never apply them near germinating seeds.

NEUTRAL SOIL—7.0 pH Most plants like to grow in slightly acid to neutral soil (6.5 to 7 pH), which can be maintained with proper mulching and fertilizing (see chapter 3).

ALKALINE SOIL—ABOVE 7.0 pH Some soils are too alkaline for plants. Weeds indicating alkalinity include white mustard, clustered bellflower, musk thistle, black knapweed, Queen-Anne's lace, salad burnet and henbane.

To Reduce Soil Alkalinity:

If soil is too alkaline, try the following:

* Add sulphur to lower the pH if it's too high for what you want to plant.
* Try adding other materials that will lower the pH, such as calcium sulphate and aluminum sulphate.
* Add compost, about 2 to 3 inches (5 to 7.5 centimetres) a year, which will make soil more neutral.

WHAT'S IN SOIL The three major elements that plants require in large quantities of soil are nitrogen, phosphorus and potassium. These are the NPK numbers on fertilizer bags—if the number is 21–7–7, that means it contains 21 percent nitrogen, and 7 percent each of phosphorus and potassium. There are vital interrelations between all the elements in the soil. Once again, it's your job to maintain the delicate balance.

The other major elements in the soil are carbon, hydrogen, oxygen, calcium, magnesium and iron. Then there are the trace elements: boron, copper, manganese, zinc, molybdenum, sulphur and zinc. These are the hardest to manipulate, so concentrate on the major elements.

Nitrogen is released when soil organisms decompose. When a plant dies, most of the nutrients taken out of the soil are returned to the soil. This in turn is transformed into humus, which contains the acids that make other nutrients available to plants. Nitrogen production increases under warm, moist conditions and slopes off under cool conditions. Nitrogen is needed for vegetative plant growth.

Organic matter in the soil is crucial for soil microorganisms to release nitrogen. Leaf mould, compost, manure, dead roots and plants, insects and animals and the minutiae of the soil—including bacteria and fungi—are all organic matter. The ultimate goal of this decaying process is the production of humus—the most superb type of organic matter you can build for your soil. When you walk through the woods, lift some moss or rotting leaves. The marvellous sticky black stuff under them is humus. The process of decomposition has been completed and it is feeding the soil. This is the material that will heal your soil if it's sick.

GREEN TIPS
SOURCES OF NITROGEN INCLUDE:

- Fish emulsion.
- Blood meal, which has a nitrogen content of 8 to 13 percent.
- Sheep manure—if you use manure to bump up the nitrogen content of your soil, I recommend sheep manure, which has a higher nitrogen content than other types. Use manure that's been composted for at least six months (the heating process will kill off any weed seeds). Manure will also improve soil texture.
- Finished compost is an excellent source of nitrogen.

The beauty of these products is that they release nitrogen slowly and naturally—usually as the plants need it. They aren't going to burn the plants or you.

On the other hand, synthetic forms of nitrogen have a much higher nitrogen content. Anhydrous ammonia is about 82 percent nitrogen. If you breathe it, you can die. If it gets too close to the root system of a plant, it causes damage. Urea has 45 percent nitrogen; if it's mishandled, plants will die. Most chemical fertilizers with high nitrogen content are taken up so quickly by a plant's root system that the plant produces

initial lush growth, which is watery and weak, more susceptible to disease and easily broken off by the wind.

Phosphorus is needed for fruit development and root
growth. It also helps plants resist disease and withstand the
stress of drought and pollution. Mix any of the following
sources of phosphorus with manure and dig in in the spring.
This nutrient doesn't leach out easily and is released into the
soil slowly.

GREEN TIPS
SOURCES OF PHOSPHORUS INCLUDE:

- Colloidal phosphate—18 to 25 percent phosphoric acid.
  Use every four years.
- Rock phosphate and greensand have long been recommended, but if they come from North America they'll
  contain uranium, which might contaminate the soil.
- Bone meal.
- Superphosphate is a rock phosphate processed with sulphuric acid. I try to keep away from products that require
  a lot of energy in their production. It also comes from
  great distances (Togo and Morocco). Find something else.
- Rock and colloidal phosphate will raise the soil pH,
  making it less acid.
- When you are using rock minerals, use them in a natural
  form. By doing this, you will avoid getting into the
  problem of excessive mineralization or the leaching of
  soluble elements, which could affect groundwater.

Potassium is needed for growth. It helps plants resist
disease and protects them from cold and from excessive loss
of water. Too much magnesium in the soil will lead to a potassium deficiency.

GREEN TIPS
SOURCES OF POTASSIUM INCLUDE:
- Wood ashes (from the fireplace, not the barbecue), but be careful—they can boost the pH, and if it gets too high, you'll kill off your acid-loving plants.
- Manure—sheep and goat manure have the highest potassium content (3 percent).
- Add straw.
- Bananas; bury banana skins near rose bushes.

Micronutrients such as manganese, iodine, zinc, iron, copper, boron and molybdenum are all in the soil and if they aren't, your plants will let you know that something is wrong. Lots of organic matter settled on top of the soil and allowed to work itself in slowly will correct any imbalances. It contains these trace elements and is the simplest, safest way to a healthy soil.

Balance is everything. When the temperature rises and the soil is moist, all these nutrients will become available to the plants much more quickly.

SOIL AMENDING

Create self-sufficient soil by making it healthy. You don't want to provide temporary solutions to any problems. Manure and organic matter aren't necessarily interchangeable in ecological gardening. Organic matter is the most important: leaves, plant waste, garden detritus, straw, hay. Straw, alas, encourages mice.

Another method of enriching the soil is to dig down and fill the hole with layers of aged leaves and manure. Earthworms do most of the work of breaking down these materials into compost.

Build up the soil with compost or make your own organic fertilizer as recommended by garden writer Eliot Coleman: 4 parts blood meal, 2 parts bone meal and 1 part kelp or rock phosphate.

Here's a good soil food recommended in the book *Organic Gardening for the Pacific Northwest*: 4 parts seed meal (or 2 parts fish meal), 1 part dolomitic limestone, 1 part rock phosphate or 1/2 part bone meal, 1 part kelp.

If you add bone and blood meal to coir, it will act as a fertilizer. Coir products are made from coconut fibre (from outer husk) and are used as an alternative to peat moss. Though I realize coir products have to be shipped long distances, that's better than destroying peat bogs.

Leaf mould is an excellent amendment. Bag leaves and place them in a corner to break down, or dig them into a big hole and let them rot, or shred them and add to the compost heap. One thing you don't do with leaves is throw them out.

Maple leaves tend to mat if you put them on the ground without letting them break down first. Since the leaves of Norway maples contain alkaloids, they should be well composted before you add them to the soil. Oak and beech are acidic and will take longer to break down than other leaves. But they are great if you are building up acid areas in your garden. Black walnut leaves contain juglone, which is toxic to many plants, so you should probably not use these leaves as soil amenders.

Extremely sandy soil is too porous and it won't support earthworms. Add masses of compost and keep adding as often as possible. Over time the soil will improve.

SOLVING SOIL PROBLEMS

If you have soil with poor texture or density, try the following:

Double dig: Dig a trench as wide as your spade, and as deep. Pile the soil from this first trench on a sheet of plastic. Loosen and amend the soil in the bottom of the trench to another spade depth. Dig another trench directly beside the first trench and put the excavated soil in the first trench; continue until you hit the last trench and then put the soil on the plastic sheet from the first in it. In all my years of gardening I have never done this, but some people swear by it.

Raised beds: Double dig the soil and add enough moistened coir and compost or manure to raise the soil at least 8 to 10 inches (20 to 25 centimetres) above ground level. Always mix coir with other soil amenders; on its own it's sterile.

LEAD IN THE SOIL: Though lead hasn't been used in paint or gasoline for some time, there is still the possibility that it might have built up in the soil, especially if you live near a parking lot or busy road. By adding lots of compost and manure, you can decrease lead absorption. By maintaining neutral soil of pH 6.5 to 7, you'll also be able to limit the build-up of lead in the soil.

ROCKY SOIL: If you have a lot of rocks on your property, you can use them in the garden. Position plants that like hot, dry conditions near large rocks. Place smooth, flat rocks near plants that like cool, moist conditions—put rocks over the roots of clematis, for instance.

BUYING SOIL

If you must buy topsoil, be careful. Try to find out where it came from. If it's from a field that was planted with corn, it may be filled with toxic chemicals. In that case, don't buy it. Of course, it is likely to have come from the nearest housing development. The valuable topsoil is removed and sold, leaving new homeowners with nothing but subsoil and clay. If you're in this situation, bump up the soil first before you go through the heartbreak of putting in a garden and watching it struggle. Use huge amounts of compost and manure to create healthy soil and keep it that way. Don't be tempted by quick solutions.

Instead of buying soil, you can prepare your own potting soil mix—particularly if you have fears about vermiculite, which may contain asbestos, in commercial mixes. A combination of clean soil, sand (builder's or horticultural sand is very gritty) and compost is a very good growing medium.

I don't mess around with soil by cultivating it once it's been planted. I like to think I'm not disturbing the complex life or delicate root systems that exist down there. After all, the most beneficial life in the soil is in the top inch (2.5 centimetres). To create a healthy, balanced soil in your ecological garden, use every alternative to cultivating that you can find. Be sure to mulch and otherwise keep the soil covered. (If you want to see what will happen when you fail to protect the soil, take a chunk of bare earth and aim your hose at it.) Return what you take from the garden *to* the garden (leaves, dead and dying plants—unless they are diseased). Feed with organic matter. Compost, compost, compost.

GREEN TIPS
SOIL LESSONS:

- Make sure you know what kind of soil and drainage you have, and work with it or amend it to accommodate the plants you want to grow. Find out what was added to your soil before you took possession. If the area has been stripped of topsoil or if chemicals have built up in the soil, you will have to improve the soil over a period of time.
- Plant when pests are less evident.
- A handy way to inoculate your soil against diseases is to plant marigolds, and then rotate them from year to year. An added bonus: rodents don't like them.

Learn to treasure the soil and approach it as a living creature rather than some dead stuff you clunk plants into. The more you are aware of the symbiosis between yourself and the soil, the more careful you will be with this miraculous substance.

SOIL TESTING

To find out where there are accredited soil testing labs in your area, Google "soil testing" plus your province or state, and you'll get an up-to-date address. When sending soil off to the lab, be sure to ask for organic solutions to any problem they find.

2

COMPOSTING

Garden Gold

My family always had a compost pile of some sort, however primitive, and I was astonished to find that this was not a universal practice. I built my first one when we bought this house in the 1960s—just as soon as we'd pulled the 2,300 square feet (213 square metres) of thigh-high weeds out of the back yard. My neighbour, objecting to what he termed "throwing out garbage and making flies," called city hall. When the health inspector arrived, he hooted with laughter, "About the only thing you're making is a lot of worms." The compost pile kept Steve and me at odds for years. We were like two politically opposed people—neither one of us could understand the other's point of view.

The value of composting has become increasingly clear. It cuts down on garbage to a huge degree. It puts back what you take out of the environment—an ideal form of recycling. And you can start any time of the year. The more I work with and read about compost, the more I realize how much

I have to learn. It's worthwhile refreshing the facts on an annual basis.

Without going on and on about its virtues, remember this: compost is even better than well-rotted manure. Manure will, of course, amend your soil beautifully, but it isn't a complete fertilizer. Compost is a much more nutritious hit for your soil. The micro-organisms that build up in it supply what is comparable in humans to an inoculation against disease or to an antibiotic if you've got a disease. Compost will improve both the aeration and drainage of your soil as it supplies nutrients. And it's free. Need I go on?

What is compost? It's organic matter broken down by bacteria and other organisms into a dark material called humus. It feels like the most perfectly wonderful soil imaginable.

To give you an idea of how easy it is to compost, consider that when you mow a lawn and leave the clippings in place, you are composting; when you let leaves stay on the ground to rot, you are composting. But to compost on a more sophisticated level, it takes a bit of effort.

* You need some form of container.
* Layer what you put into it.
* Keep it relatively moist (not wet).
* Turn it occasionally.

If you follow these simple rules, you will have good compost and it won't smell. What creates a stink is throwing in all of one thing: nothing but kitchen waste, nothing but leaves, nothing but grass clippings. Gases build up, ergo, nasty smell. By layering, the stack heats up and cooks the smell out. I can get quite intoxicated by compost odour. When it has a slight earthy smell, which I love, that means it's a success. It's a sensual pleasure to let the lovely stuff run through your fingers.

The scientific basis of all composting is that organic matter is valuable only while decaying, and even finished compost still has a way to go in that process. It's this decomposition process that provides nutrients to the soil. Microscopic bacteria and other minuscule organisms continually assimilate organic material, releasing the nutrients plants need. Bacteria alone are 60 percent protein, and they provide food for the munchers you can see: worms, insects such as sowbugs, nematodes, mites and so on. They eat, digest, excrete and die. As this happens, more and more nutrients are released. All that life, the visible and invisible, the creepies and crawlies in your compost—talk about teeming with life—is working for you.

The red worms that develop in compost heaps are special worms that don't live in the earth. They are smaller and live only in compost, creating air passages and providing the environment for the oxygen-loving organisms. When compost heats up during the decomposition process, they won't die or scurry away. And they seem to appear like magic once you provide the right kind of environment for them.

There are two types of decaying processes: aerobic and anaerobic:

Aerobic composting is when there's enough air to feed oxygen-loving bacteria and spur them on with the work of decomposition.

Aerobic is the best and most efficient, but it means you need to get oxygen into the heap by turning it. Leave a post in the centre to wiggle, or use any ingenious method you can think of to stir up the mix.

Anaerobic is without air; decay is slower; gases are formed and probably the pile will end up smelling like rotten eggs. Anaerobic composting is primarily carried on in closed bins or silos.

LOCATION

A compost heap needs good drainage, so don't build it on top of concrete or in an area where water won't run off. Give it a shady spot so it won't dry out, but place it where the sun might hit it at some time, though this is not terribly important. Use a cover to keep animals out, and keep the heap as damp as a squeezed-out sponge—neither soggy nor dry.

An excellent place to locate a compost bin or pile is about 6 feet (2 metres) away from a birch or elder tree. Worms adore both these trees.

HOW TO GET STARTED

Use the container that suits the size of your garden best. I have a relatively small garden, so I have a double-sided affair like the one illustrated. You can buy plastic composters but can also build your own unit cheaply with used materials in the following way:

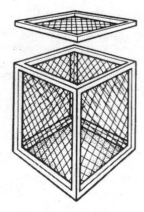 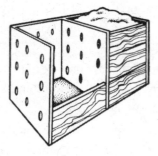

Two examples of homemade compost bins: (left) This single bin is particularly useful for the preparation of leaf mould. (right) The double bin has holes drilled in the sides to allow air to circulate.

IF SPACE IS A PROBLEM For balconies and small city gardens: poke a bunch of small holes in the sides of a plastic garbage can and keep your kitchen wastes and plant clippings in there. Roll it around occasionally to keep the material inside suitably mingled and aerated. A 30-gallon (120-litre) plastic garbage container with firm-locking lid and wheels will be even easier to move into place.

IF SPACE ISN'T A PROBLEM Install two bins: you can use one for holding materials until you're ready to layer them, and the other for the actual compost pile. You can also try the following:

- Have a compost bin for kitchen wastes (plus clippings, and the formula below) and another larger one for leaves and garden detritus. Stockpile and keep adding layer by layer.
- To make the layering easier, keep a garbage container beside the composter. Put chopped-up garden discards in it and use this to cover kitchen scraps. I turn the pile every five days and attempt to be fairly scrupulous about what's in each layer.

As far as I'm concerned, you can't have too many compost piles, especially if the garden has lots of trees and shrubs. I get an average of twenty large bags of leaves and I recycle every one plus any that I can nab from the street when neighbours throw them out.

There is another quite interesting composter available (and a Canadian invention at that) called the Green Cone. It has an open basket bottom that is put into a 20-inch (50-centimetre) hole. The cone is placed on top and tightly sealed—this keeps animals out. You can dump everything into it, including meat and fish bones and things that don't break down in an ordinary composter (eggshells, for example, which seem to last a millennium). Water is drawn out of the waste by the earth around it, reducing about 70 to 90 percent of the matter. The rest gradually disappears. It's cleared out once a year.

We now have municipal organic-waste collection in our city, which means that all food scraps can be put in a green bin by the curb. What with recycling and refusing to buy over-packaged goods, we are down to a small bag of garbage every two weeks.

STUFF FOR THE COMPOST PILE

You need about a cubic yard (cubic metre) of material to begin a compost heap. If you don't have this much, go straight to vermicomposting (see page 31). To get started, it is possible to buy commercial activators—compost accelerators they are usually called. Save your money. They aren't necessary if you have a good mix of materials to compost, which will also provide the most nutrients for plants. Some completed compost, good garden soil, a sprinkling of blood meal or chopped-up nettles will perform as activators. The finer the grind of everything in the heap, the faster the decomposition process will be.

GREEN TIPS
WHAT TO PUT IN YOUR COMPOST PILE:

- Grass clippings that haven't been poisoned with herbicides.
- Chopped-up leaves; if you have space for an acid compost, use oak and beech, but they will take much longer to break down.
- Anything from the garden such as weeds (no seeds please), stems chopped up; tomato and squash vines.
- Sawdust, ground-up wood chips and nutshells, coffee grounds, blood meal.

- Kitchen wastes, cut up fine or run through a food processor with a little water (this is a good way to add moisture to the heap).
- Manure.
- Coir—this won't add any nutrients to the heap but will lighten the texture.
- Leaf mould.
- Wood ashes from the fireplace.
- Feathers.
- Lint from the dryer.
- Corn cobs, although they are really slow to break down.
- Shredded paper (no glossy or waxed surfaces).
- Hair—your own or your pet's.
- Shredded-up newspapers—even the colour sections are now printed with vegetable-based inks.

WHAT TO AVOID IN YOUR COMPOST PILE:

- Meat, bones, cheese and all other dairy products.
- Anything from the barbecue.
- Cat and dog feces—too tricky (there was a salmonella outbreak in British Columbia traced to vegetables grown in compost that contained cat feces).
- Absolutely any garden clippings or plants that have had pesticides, herbicides or any other toxic chemicals sprayed on them.
- Anything sick or blighted.
- Anything that isn't biodegradable.

LAYERING THE COMPOST PILE

When I first composted, I just made a pile and tossed stuff on it until it seemed big enough. Then I left it alone until it was ready to use—in a year or so—and moved on to another area. Once I started making layers of different kinds of material, things speeded up dramatically. It took a while before I realized that a container makes a big difference; that all the stuff from the garden should be cut up as small as possible; and that it needed to be dampened down slightly. Slow learner, I guess. It certainly wasn't lack of interest; I had enough piles to always have some compost ready to spread around.

About this business of cutting everything up in tiny pieces—my neighbours Amanda and Laurie and I bought a chipper/shredder together many years ago. We geared ourselves up in the recommended goggles, leather gloves and huge earmuff-style protectors—this should tell you something about the noise. It was incredible. Terrifying. Sure we got good stuff, but what we did to the air around us suddenly didn't seem worth it.

How often did we use it? Well, that was it—once. It was a hideously expensive experiment and the ridiculous thing didn't even chop up leaves. Yet my friend Tim bought a really expensive, heavy-duty chipper/shredder and he swears by it. If you are going to buy one, get a large enough group together to go for the big one and make it a community effort. I've heard of using a Whipper Snipper in a plastic garbage container to chop up leaves. But that is another screaming electric machine. Some people pile up leaves and run an electric lawn mower over them. Use a grass catcher to contain the leaves or you'll have shreds all over the place.

Me? I'm making do with heavy clippers to cut up the outside stuff and an old food processor to chop up the kitchen stuff. Noise and air pollution have to be considered as well as the benefits of what you're putting into the soil.

HOW TO LAYER

Compost piles need air, heat and moisture. Three by 3 feet (90 by 90 centimetres) is about the minimum size for a pile or bin. Four by 4 feet (1.2 by 1.2 metres) is good, but a bigger pile of 5 to 6 feet (1.5 to 1.8 metres) is even better.. An effective compost must have layers of different materials. Just throwing in all your kitchen wastes or all leaves will not work quickly and will end up smelling terrible because of anaerobic action. By having it properly aired, you'll help eliminate any smells. During the process of decomposition, carbon dioxide is given off (it's odourless) and nitrogen stays about the same if the pile is balanced. Parasites, pests, seeds and diseases are burned off in the heating process.

Make the first layer out of relatively large chunky material such as twiggy clippings to aerate the bottom of the pile. I always build mine straight on the soil so that worms and microbes can find their way into the pile as quickly as possible. I lose a few nutrients this way—they leach into the soil—but not enough to be a worry.

Think green and brown, and make each layer about 6 inches (15 centimetres) thick, but this isn't a rigid rule. Composting should be fun—not painful measuring.

Green stuff: Kitchen wastes, grass clippings, healthy plant detritus.

Brown stuff: Manure, soil, blood meal.

Moisten the lot and turn it in a few days to mix it up. Have something to aerate the pile, something you can wiggle around in the middle to get oxygen in there. Any kind of tube or metal pipe will work. If the pile seems a bit slow to heat up, speed things up with a sprinkling of blood meal, a hoof and horn meal mixture or manure. Or pour manure tea (manure that's been sitting in a bucket of water for a week) over the top.

HOT ROT

To use this method, you must think beyond mere layering to the nitrogen:carbon ratio. You want the pile to hit a high of 160°F (70°C) to kill off any insect eggs, larvae, parasites, weed seeds, diseases—all the things you don't want to spread around the garden. Basic components of the pile are:

Nitrogen: Without nitrogen, things get off to a very slow start indeed; it's the most important ingredient in the compost pile. The high nitrogen content in manure, green plants and grass acts to heat up the pile. Chicken manure is especially high in nitrogen, as are blood meal, tea leaves, peanut shells, bone meal, urine (human or animal, diluted with three parts water—how you get this is your problem, just use your imagination), feathers, wool wastes, green plants and grass clippings.

Potassium: Wood ashes (don't use this if you are spreading the compost around vegetables; there's too much of a build-up of heavy metals), water lily stems, urine (diluted with three parts water), oak leaves, banana peels, fruit tree leaves.

Phosphorus: Rock phosphate, bone meal, blood meal, wool wastes, marine products such as kelp. These materials will conserve the nitrogen in the pile.

Trace minerals: Rock dusts, marine products such as kelp.

Carbon: Old leaves, hay, sawdust, dried grass, weeds, paper and straw. These should all be slightly damp when added to the pile.

Recommended ratio: Soil expert Dr. Stuart B. Hill says that the ideal ratio of carbon to nitrogen is from 35:1 to 30:1.

How do you know if you haven't got this ratio? The pile won't heat up.

If you compost in a container, it's easy to mix by eye. Kitchen wastes can be allowed to accumulate in a garbage pail until you're ready to put them in the compost.

Composting is an ad hoc learning experience and you should end up doing it almost by instinct. If the pile is wet enough and still doesn't heat up, you haven't got enough nitrogen. The easiest remedy is to sprinkle some blood meal on top. If you've got too much nitrogen, then it'll smell like ammonia.

When my pile doesn't smell earthy, I just throw some soil on top and this seems to right things almost immediately. It's also a good way to top off the pile. A day or so later, the pile will heat up and continue heating up for a couple of weeks. Then, turn the whole heap over.

Turning the pile is made much easier if you have two bins and all you have to do is move decaying stuff from one to the other. If not, you'll have to work in your own small space. Turning blends the pile as well as aerating it.

THE 14-DAY COMPOSTING METHOD
Encyclopedia of Organic Gardening:
1. Shred everything going into the pile, keeping the carbon/nitrogen ratio 30 to 1. Mix after shredding and put into a pile not more than 5 feet (1.5 metres) high.
2. Moisten material evenly without making it soggy.
3. Leave for 3 days. Make sure it is heating up. Then turn every 2 days.
4. You can use it in 2, maybe 3, weeks..

With this, you lose fewer nutrients. The compost won't be perfectly decomposed, but you can use it around the garden as the decaying process continues.

COMPOST AND CHEMICALS
The question most often asked of composting experts is, what about all those chemicals applied to our food? How will

this affect the compost? What about composting kitchen wastes that haven't been grown organically? By using a brown/green mixture in the compost, you can allay some of these concerns—the heat generated by a properly balanced carbon-to-nitrogen ratio will break things down. But there are hundreds of pesticides registered for use on food crops. Some of these pesticides can remain in the soil for years without breaking down. If you're worried—or if you put a lot of potato or fruit peels in your compost—by all means have it tested. Some tests have shown that approximately 74 percent of poisons such as 2,4-D remained even after a year of composting; with others, such as the insecticide lindane, anywhere from 55 to 99 percent remained in the compost.

It's time to switch to organically grown food whenever it's available. Obviously, when you grow your own, you won't have to worry. I belong to a food co-operative and that's part of our business—searching out farmers and suppliers who grow food without chemicals. Organically grown food tastes a lot better than most supermarket stuff anyway. Read labels carefully. The symbol of the Canadian Organic Growers is a horn of plenty. One of their standards is that only soil that has not been treated chemically for at least 5 years can be certified as organic. Given the half-life of most pesticides, this is an absolute must. There are now more than 15,000 people growing organic food commercially in Canada (though only a few thousand are certified). Join a Community Supported Agriculture (CSA) program where you pay a farmer to grow your food.

EARTHWORM TEA

You can make excellent compost by raising earthworms in a trash can. Earthworm castings are incredibly rich in nutrients.

- Take an uncovered 21-gallon (80-litre) plastic trash can and insert a plastic spigot about 6 inches (15 centimetres) from the bottom.
- Fill the can with a mix of garden soil, grass clippings, leaves and partially decayed fruit or vegetable scraps.
- Add enough water so the worms can live comfortably in decaying vegetable matter above the water line. Worms produce nutrient-rich castings as they digest the organic matter.
- Wash water down over the compost and castings and extract from the bottom. Add the same amount of water to the can that you draw off. Plug up the plastic spigot.
- By adding more water you drive the worms and other useful chewing insects back to the top. And the cycle begins again.

WORM COMPOSTING Vermicomposting is ideal for those of us who live in the north, or in apartments, and want to continue to recycle kitchen scraps all winter. Use red worms, which are thinner than earthworms. They eat their own weight in organic matter daily, and you'll get finished stuff in 2 to 3 months.

GREEN TIPS
LET WORMS EAT YOUR GARBAGE

- Keep the container indoors during the winter so that you can keep composting all year long. You do not want your worms to freeze. Since they are odourless and won't squirm all over your floors—they hate being exposed to the light—you don't run any risk in this venture.
- Use a box (wood or plastic) with a lid. The worms need a dark, moist place in which to live.

- Add straw, manure, leaves, shredded newsprint, cardboard or grass clippings as bedding material. You can bury kitchen detritus in this material.
- Take red worms from your outdoor compost pile or order them from a commercial supplier.
- When castings (the dark stuff) are ready, move the castings to one side of the bin and make a new bed on the other side—the worms will migrate to the new area and you can harvest your finished castings.

In her book *Worms Eat My Garbage,* the late Mary Appelhof recommends a container 12 inches (30 centimetres) deep, 2 feet (60 centimetres) wide, and 3 feet (90 centimetres) long. Make sure there are holes for air.

The Rodale Encyclopedia recommends a box 2 feet (60 centimetres) to 3 feet (90 centimetres) square, and 2 feet (60 centimetres) high. Use a mix of weeds, leaves, grass clippings, 15 percent manure and 12 percent topsoil; kitchen scraps can substitute for manure. Mix thoroughly and put in box. Buy red worms. If the mix is too hot, add water before adding worms. Keep watered, but not soggy. For the best compost, you want a good combination of worms, bacteria and fungi.

COLD WEATHER COMPOSTING

You can make this in fall and allow it to overwinter. The heap will be ready by spring. Pile size is the key because extreme cold or excessive moisture slow the process down—the larger the pile, the better the insulation. The outermost layer of organic material will provide protection. Make it as big as 4 feet (1.2 metres) high, 7 feet (2.1 metres) wide, and 14 feet (4.2 metres) long, or as small as 4 feet (1.2 metres) by 6 feet (1.8 metres) by 7 feet (2.1 metres). If you start it smack in the middle of the garden, it will feed the soil below. Covering it with black plastic will speed things along. This method can work to -5°F (-20°C). The outer layers freeze, but thaw quickly.

Make separate piles of material—garden waste, leaves, straw, manure—and let them get dampened by fall rain. Then spread the stuff out to dry. Alternate 1-inch (2.5-centimetre) layers; any unshredded garden waste will provide air pockets. Make into a long flat rectangle. Three weeks later, once the pile has cooled down, turn and mix the wet areas with dry, and break up any clumps. At this stage, minimize the surface area and make a rounded mound as tall as possible. Let sit until needed in spring. Scatter worms throughout pile. They'll keep on digesting all winter. Raw materials shrink by about 50 percent, leaving 15 cubic yards (11 cubic metres) of winter compost.

SIMPLE WINTER COMPOSTING: I put spare leaves into plastic bags, dampen them slightly and add a little soil and manure. I leave them piled up and occasionally toss them around. By spring, they are in good enough shape to be used as leaf mould.

For regular compost, save a bag or so of leaves, and store some dirt in a garage or shed to keep it from freezing. Carry on putting kitchen wastes in your bin, and add the leaves and soil when you think it's necessary—you'll be supplying nitrogen from the scraps, and carbon from the leaves. In spring, this stuff will really compost quickly.

ACID COMPOST: This can be useful if you are bumping up the acidity in sections of the garden. Chop up oak leaves and stuff them into a garbage bag, slightly dampened. Add soil and manure and roll the bag around to mix. Use it in spring around acid-loving plants.

BAG COMPOSTING: My Auntie Marge used to do the following: she kept all her fruit and vegetable peelings, tea bags and so on in a small plastic bag at the side of the sink. As soon as the bag was full, she put water in it, tied the ends together, put it in a nice shady spot under a tree and then made a slit down the middle. Everything inside gradually rotted and there was no smell at all. Worms got inside and did their work. She piled lawn clippings and other garden rubbish on top of the bags—just so no one would complain. In February (she lived on the West Coast), she dug a trench, filled it with the contents of a few bags and planted her peas.

COMPOSTING PET WASTE

A word about dog and cat feces—don't, as some advise, put them in the compost. They may have parasites that won't do anyone any good. There are commercial recycling bins designed especially for dog and cat poo. They are designed almost like nesting boxes with the feces on top, worms attacking them and the results dropping below. Another is like a plastic garbage can with holes in the side that you sink into the ground. Active enzymes are added to break down the feces. Most of the ones advertised on the Web guarantee that they are childproof and most are small enough to work in any garden.

Here's a do-it-yourself method. In a well-drained place, but not near tree roots, dig a hole 1 1/2 feet (.5 metres) deep, 12 inches (30 centimetres) wide. Take a plastic bucket with holes punched in it near the top and with a secure lid, and put it in the hole. Tuck stones or gravel down the outside of the bucket. Put in the dog or cat droppings, add half a box of septic starter and 4 cups (1 litre) of water. Wait a couple of days, then add feces every day. Pour in a bucket of water once a week and a packet of septic starter once or twice a month. The liquid created oozes through the holes near the rim.

GREEN TIPS

- Comfrey grows fast and spreads like crazy. Keep chopping it back to contain it, and put the bits into the compost. It adds as much nitrogen as manure.
- Stinging nettle contains iron and also speeds up decay.
- Yarrow adds trace elements to the compost.
- All those sowbugs you see in the compost aren't yucky— they are very effective at breaking up the decaying matter. You want to encourage a diversity of animal life in the compost—except for rats, mice and raccoons, of course.

COMPOST PROBLEMS

Flies: If you see flies buzzing around, add a layer of soil and be sure to bury fruit and kitchen material.

Rotten egg odour: This means the pile is anaerobic—too wet and not enough air. It will smell awful, especially on a warm summer's day. You've got to get some air in there. Turn the pile daily for a few days and add something absorbent like a little soil.

Ammonia odour: Too much nitrogen—add carbon (straw, sawdust, leaves, newspapers), then turn the pile to let gas escape.

Other bad odour: It will also smell if you haven't got a good enough mix of materials. Too much of any one element just doesn't work properly. Keep the green-brown layers in mind.

Too dry: If the heap is too dry, it may mean it's just too big. You'll probably have to re-sort the layers and dampen them down.

Too cool: If it isn't heating up, it means you need nitrogen. Here's the nitrogen list again: blood meal, kitchen scraps, fresh manure (not an easy commodity to find in the middle of the city, but terrific if you have access to a farm), fresh grass clippings that have not been treated with a herbicide.

Heating unevenly: If the pile is warm and moist only in the middle, it's probably too small. Add more well-moistened material.

FINISHED COMPOST: Well-prepared, finished compost has a crumbly texture like humus. If it doesn't, put it through a coarse sieve and toss the unfinished material back into the compost for another go. It should be quite dark and have a pleasant smell.

HOW TO USE COMPOST:
- Compost, like any soil amender, can be dug into the earth, but I much prefer to use it as top or side dressing around a plant so as not to disturb the soil.
- It loosens up clay soil, retains water in sand and adds essential nutrients.
- It's classified as a soil conditioner rather than a fertilizer, but compost provides trace elements on a time-release basis better than anything else does.
- Use it everywhere, including as part of a seed-starting mix.

COMPOST TEA: This is a surprisingly effective way to make a little compost go a long way. Just pour water over a porous bag filled with compost and leave it for a week in a large container. Dilute it by half with more water if it seems to be getting very strong. You can even add some manure. Quite often I just put a shovel full of compost in a pail, fill it with hot water and swish it around. When it cools off, it's ready to use.

You can be as casual or as complicated as you want about your composting—just don't throw out material that can be returned to the earth. Don't get trapped into competitive composting. It is such a pain to go to a party and hear people trying to one-up each other about the quality of their compost. This is supposed to be good for you as well as your garden.

3

MULCHING AND FERTILIZING

To Feed and Protect

WHY MULCH?

Mulching seems to be a baffling garden subject. A lot of people don't bother. But think of the soil with the same kind of tenderness you do your own skin. Almost automatically you protect it from sun, wind and lashing rain. Soil needs exactly the same treatment. Mulching is the answer. It means covering the earth to shield it from crippling damage by the sun, to keep it moisturized and to prevent weeds from growing in the wrong place. In winter, plants are cossetted by mulch, which also feeds the soil as it breaks down.

Sounds like a magic hit, right? There's more. It will save you a tonne of work. Weeding is reduced to practically nothing when you mulch. You won't disturb tender root systems by cultivating because mulching eliminates that chore. Soil temperatures remain moderate because mulch keeps the soil cool during the day and warm at night.

It gets better. A good mulch will help feed the ever-valuable earthworms because it adds a wide spectrum of nutrients to the soil during decomposition. It helps to keep the soil from becoming compacted, thereby messing up the lives of bacteria and other good organisms.

In the forest, whatever falls to the ground eventually decomposes to become humus. This rich, black organic material is the lifeline of the natural world. What we do with mulching serves much the same function. Even when there is a drought, a layer of mulch will continue to provide food for the soil and keep it relatively cool and moist. Any kind of mulch will help to reduce the amount of water needed because it cuts down on evaporation and holds moisture in the ground where it's needed.

There has to be a downside to all this, of course. Mulch can become home to slugs, earwigs and other little beasts. But you can easily shove the mulch to one side, pick out the offending creatures, then cover up again. I tend not to worry about what's going on under there, though. Think of mulch as a way to trap pests and improve your attitude immeasurably.

The final argument for mulching is that it will probably keep diseases at bay. According to Dr. Hill, microbial toxins released during mulch decomposition help control disease; as well, certain nematode-destroying fungi are encouraged by soil conditions under the mulch.

Commercially bagged mulch is available but it's expensive. It's easy to make your own and that way you'll know exactly what you are putting on the soil and near your plants.

HOW TO MULCH

It's important to mulch in spring, through the growing season and then again after the ground has frozen. You can mulch once plants are established as long as you don't let it touch any new growth of the stems. This is generally a good practice—you don't want to cut off oxygen to the plants or set up any conditions whereby new plant growth can rot easily. It's becoming a regular practice to mulch right up and around perennials and they don't seem to suffer. But it's still a good idea to keep mulch away from woody parts of stems to avoid rot. Another good idea is to use a thin layer of finely shredded material rather than a whole lot of loose unshredded stuff in mulch.

GENERAL MULCHING PRACTICES:
* First, prepare the soil, plant as usual and level with a rake.
* Spread a layer of manure, leaf mould and compost over the surface of the evenly raked soil.
* Plants that need a deep mulch for winter protection should have a mulch layer 3 inches (7.5 centimetres) thick. Put it on once frost persists during the day. Mulch moderates soil temperatures, keeping them even, which will help prevent the ravages of freeze-thaw cycles that rip plants right out of the ground.
* Remove winter mulch in spring and toss it straight into the compost, where it will continue to break down. Then reapply as needed during the spring and right into summer.

MULCHING PROBLEMS:
I've talked to people who are afraid to mulch because they've managed to kill off plants by doing so. It usually turns out that they put mulch on when the ground was too soggy or too dry. This is especially dangerous when you've got young transplants. Don't mulch until the plants show new growth.
* Don't let mulch touch the base of any woody plant.

- Never mulch on waterlogged soils—air won't be able to reach the soil. You also run the risk of your plants developing mould.
- Never mulch on bone-dry soils—it will draw out whatever small amount of moisture there is in the soil.

WHAT TO USE AS MULCH

My favourite mulch is 1 part compost, 1 part sheep manure and 1 part coir mixed up with ground-up leaves.

Here is a partial list of materials you can use for mulch:

- Leaves are just about the best thing you can use. Shred them as finely as possible or use unshredded ones mixed with straw.
- Evergreen boughs, pine needles: beg, borrow or steal as much as you can. They will also protect small shrubs from fierce winter winds. They are especially welcomed by acid-loving plants.
- Grass clippings, untouched by herbicides, can be left on your lawn after mowing—this is still mulching. But you can also clear them off once or twice a year to use as an activator in your compost pile if it isn't heating up.
- Pine cones look attractive and allow moisture to get through. But they are a pain in the neck if you have great piles of leaves landing on them—it's impossible to rake them off. They are most effective under large shrubs and away from deciduous trees such as maples.
- Straw and hay are excellent protection against the drying winter winds. Spread layers several inches (8 centimetres) thick over empty beds. When you're ready to plant, pull the material aside and proceed as usual. Make sure neither contains any seeds. Add compost to the soil before using these as mulches.

- Coffee grounds and tea leaves can be recycled as mulch especially around acid-loving plants.
- Shredded newspaper is quite effective. Most newspaper inks no longer contain lead; even colour sections are printed with clay-based inks. However, avoid the glossy magazine sections.
- Marble chips.
- Mixed tree trimmings shredded as fine as possible.
- Seaweed.
- Composted rice hulls, buckwheat hulls.
- Shells from the following nuts: almonds, pecans, hazelnuts, peanuts.
- Stones.
- Weeds and anything else from the vegetable garden can be cut up and used as mulch, as long as you've made sure there are no seeds. If this doesn't suit you aesthetically, put a layer of manure, or something similar, on top. I prefer to put them in the compost, but they're terrific mulches if you're short of material.
- You can use corn cobs ground up into 1-inch (2.5-centimetre) pieces, but add blood meal, cottonseed meal, bone meal or compost underneath.
- Salt hay grows in the marshy lands near the sea. It is excellent if you are lucky enough to have access to such an area.
- Sawdust can be used, but add soybean meal, cottonseed meal or compost to the soil before mulching. Be warned, however, that this may attract mice. You could add poison—I wouldn't. Make sure this mulch is not near plants that mice like to gnaw on.
- Cedar bark, wood chips and wood wastes look good and allow moisture to seep through. However, they should be

finely chopped and partially composted before you apply them as mulch.

- Discarded fabrics such as old rags, wool or cotton castoffs.
- Shredded unbleached paper such as the kind used in coffee filters.
- Black plastic is often recommended and though it does have many uses, I'm not crazy about anything that requires a lot of processing energy or is synthetic. Besides, it adds nothing to the soil.

GREEN TIPS
HOW TO USE COMPOST AS MULCH:

- If you have very fine compost, you can apply it to the soil before you plant. The closer to planting time, the finer the grind should be. To get this, push the compost through a sieve and then throw the remainder back into the heap.
- Once the ground is frozen in fall, use whatever is left in the compost bin as a mulch around plants. Don't worry if it looks a little raw—it will continue to decompose.
- Mix compost and soil and use as a side dressing. It won't burn the plants. Do this a couple of times a year.
- Compost can even be used around acid-loving plants, but it's best to make an acid compost (see page 33).
- For plants in pots, mix 1 part compost with 2 parts soil and run it through a screen. Add a 1-inch (2.5-centimetre) layer to the top of the soil.

LEAVES AS MULCH: Never, ever get rid of your leaves, even if your area has a public composting plan. The smallest garden will probably have a corner in which to store leaves while they break down into leaf mould. In the long run, leaves are more valuable to your garden than manure—and a lot cheaper. They combine carbon, minerals, nitrogen, phosphorus, calcium, magnesium and water to make food for next year's plant growth. As leaves break down, humus is produced, which improves the soil and makes it more moisture-retentive.

Shred leaves to help them break down more quickly. Dried leaves can be raked over perennial beds for winter protection. Be cautious here. Some leaves, such as maple, will form a thick mat once they are wet. This can smother plants, undoing whatever good the mulch is supposed to provide. In spring, rake them off and put them into the compost or other piles to further break down.

I have one small section of the garden where I throw all sorts of biggish stuff like woody stems, chunky plants and extra leaves. I chop them up as much as I can and twice a year turn the pile over. I don't expect much useable material out of this for a couple of years. In another small area, I dig a hole, put down an 18-inch (45-centimetre) layer of leaves, dampen slightly, then add a layer of manure combined with soil. The manure provides nitrogen, which begins the process of decay. I keep doing this until there's a reasonable pile—though it's never reasonable enough because I always seem to have bags of leaves left over. It's topped off with a layer of soil. This breaks down slowly into leaf mould, which I distribute around the garden the following year. Leaf mould such as this will hold up to ten times the moisture of regular soil.

Bag up the leftover leaves (I grab anyone else's I can snag), make them moist but not soggy, add some manure and soil. By spring it's astonishing how much this has decomposed. My composting companion, Amanda, also collects leaves that others put out. She piles bags full of them over her pond to form a layer of protection for her fish. In spring, the leaves go into the composter or, if they've broken down enough, are distributed over new beds.

Leaves taught me a great lesson years ago. One area of the garden was turned into part of a basketball court for the kids. Once they left home, I had the surface removed and found not a worm in what looked like dead dirt. For a few years, I threw all the leaves from the garden into that area. Then I started turning it over, adding manure and now I've got worms and plants flourishing there. I once called it the *Jardin de refusee*; today it's one of the loveliest parts of the garden.

GREEN TIPS

MAKE THE MOST OF LEAVES

- Chopped-up leaves can be used alone or mixed with pretty well any other mulch, except stones.
- Mulch your rhododendrons and other acid-loving plants with oak leaves or pine needles.
- Be sure to rake large maple leaves off lawns and beds since they tend to form a mat once they are wet. Let them break down into leaf mould first.

PEAT MOSS AS MULCH: Once again we're in an area of controversy. Bogs are home to wildlife and unique plant communities. As we strip these bogs of peat, we're also slowly eroding our wetlands, which are as important to the climate as the rain forests. Bogs grow at a rate of .04 of an inch (1 millimetre) a year, so when people talk about peat moss being a renewable resource, they are not referring to our lifetime.

According to the peat moss industry, there are 270 million acres (109 million hectares) of peat bogs (about 25 percent of the world's total). According to *Harrowsmith* magazine, bogs cover 425,000 square miles (1 million square kilometres)— about 12 percent of our total land mass. Of this, 10 to 20 percent is useable. Canadian peat bogs have been forming for more than 10,000 years and some of them are now 20 to 30 feet (6 to 9 metres) deep. It takes about 300 years to create a foot (30 centimetres) of peat moss. You have to consult your conscience about continuing to use peat. These bogs are home to millions of plants and insects, and to harvest the peat requires draining valuable wetlands. Think about all of this the next time you buy a bale of peat. And also remember that peat bogs store carbon; once the peat is harvested and dried out, this carbon is released into the atmosphere.

As I've mentioned, I've now switched to coir products instead of using peat moss. I use them mainly in containers to make the soil more moisture-retentive. I'll continue this until I find out that something ghastly is going on with coir products. You have to be vigilant about all of this stuff.

NEWSPAPER AS MULCH: After you've seeded an area, wet the soil and cover the ground with dampened newspapers. Keep checking on whether the seeds are germinating and whether they need water. Once the seedlings start to sprout, fold the paper so it acts as a mulch between plants.

Rake it off in the spring to let the soil warm up. It can also be added to the compost to break down even further.

To extend a border, use about 10 layers of well-dampened newspaper and leave in place. You can plant in a few weeks if it's kept damp. Just slit the newspaper and pop in the plant. Cover the newspaper with a layer of soil and manure to keep it from blowing away.

CREATIVE MULCHING: Your true designer mulch can make a garden look clean and tidy and give it a consistent look between lashings of colour from plants and shrubs. It can be effective in keeping plants from getting splashed by heavy rains.

Designer mulch: I like to use a combination of compost and ground-up leaves or leaf mould with a topping of manure. It turns a pleasant greyish brown and looks very neat.

Stone mulching: In some borders, a stone mulch looks perfect. The stones heat up quickly in spring and keep warm at night. Cultivate the soil deeply and add lots of organic matter. Top off with a layer of stones (3/4-inch/19-millimetre pea gravel looks handsome). This is particularly good for alpine plants since it echoes the original habitat in which many of them grow.

Living mulches: You can create a truly aesthetic soil cover by planting a living mulch. This can be a ground cover, a spreading shrub or ornamental grasses. It will keep the soil intact, provide a floor for your garden and add colour, texture and warmth. This also has the virtue of adding diversity to the garden. A collection of thymes, for instance, has a sensual tapestry effect.

FERTILIZING

I have never used chemical fertilizers partly because I didn't understand the NPK (nitrogen, phosphorus, potassium) stuff on the labels. Eventually I avoided them because it just didn't seem logical to pay a lot of money for fertilizers when compost could do the trick *el cheapo*. I didn't realize at first that the basis of all organic gardening is to "feed the soil, not the plant." It's an aphorism worth repeating and makes great sense. Once you've got the healthiest soil possible, it is simple to keep it that way. What you do in the ecological garden is imitate nature as closely as possible. Since soil comprises minerals and humus, it seems sensible to use rock fertilizers for mineralization and organic material that will break down into humus.

A healthy soil contains just about every element that plants need: nitrogen, phosphorus and potassium; zinc, manganese, boron, iron, sulphur, copper, magnesium, molybdenum, chlorine; and lots of organic matter and humus. It will be well drained, friable and easy to work.

Fertilizers are absorbed by the plant's root system and provide the extra nutrients the plant may require. An organic fertilizer feeds as it decomposes. The rate of decomposition depends on the temperature, moisture and pH of the soil. Fertilizers are the food for all the large and small organisms in the soil. You want to treat them as well as you treat yourself— with a balanced diet. And just like all diets, they vary.

Organic fertilizers provide the same nutrients as inorganic fertilizers and since they are made with plant, animal and mineral sources, they are returning what came from the earth to the earth. The nutrients in inorganic fertilizers come from sources other than living matter or ones that don't have a carbon structure. These synthetics rush to the roots immediately. If you add too much, you run the risk of root burn. Since the nature of plants is still such a mystery even to trained scientists, we poor souls without that kind of background aren't necessarily going to make the perfect choices for our plants.

Your soil can be tested to see if you have any major nutrients missing, but usually the condition of your plants will let you know this. The pH of your soil is going to influence how nutrients are absorbed.

Fertilizer is any material that gives the plant nutrients for development and growth. Organic matter is matter that will break down, decay and, in the process, feed the soil.

- A complete fertilizer contains nitrogen, phosphorus and potassium.
- An incomplete fertilizer has only one or two of these elements.
- To understand fertilizer analysis, you must know that 20–10–5, for example, means there is 20 percent nitrogen, 10 percent phosphorus, 5 percent potassium. It's all relative—20–10–5 contains four times as much nitrogen as potassium, twice as much phosphorus, that is, a ratio of 4–2–1.

All living matter, plant or animal, is composed of compounds with carbon structure. Proteins, fats, carbohydrates and other compounds synthesized by an organism have one common factor, a carbon structure. Truly organic fertilizers must consist of nutrient elements derived from compounds with a carbon structure. Any of the following is an organic fertilizer when placed in the soil—manure, bone meal and chopped garden detritus. These will provide a slow-release, non-burning source of nutrition. The nutrients will stay in the soil rather than leach out. Anything organic will eventually provide the wonder of wonders—humus, which will, in turn, improve any soil.

THE CHEMICALS: Be wary of the company that will inevitably come around to fertilize your property (for lots of money) with synthetic "organic" fertilizers—more chemicals.

Chemical fertilizers are the magic bullets that really only serve to give an instant boost. It's the long-term effects you must be wary about. These fertilizers destroy all the important living creatures in the soil, especially earthworms. The soil itself becomes less friable. Chemicals prevent some plants from absorbing nutrients. And, of course, since these chemicals are water-soluble, they will eventually leach into the ground water and also muck up our streams, rivers and lakes. Some of the chemicals zip through the soil like the proverbial dose of salts. They go so swiftly that they don't pause long enough to help out the plants. Others accumulate in the soil and really mess things up. If they become concentrated, they can react with clay to form a hardpan—through which no water can move.

You can't necessarily anticipate the chemical reaction that a synthetic will have with your particular soil. Your plants depend on a balanced supply of nutrients. And it's this balance that is so important. Plants can't screen out ionized chemicals and so are in danger of becoming saturated with unbalanced materials.

One side effect of chemicals—killing off beneficial organisms—can destroy the fertility of your soil.

As I've said before, earthworms are our friends. Without them, the soil becomes infertile. They can clean up a garden by ingesting 90 percent of the leaves that fall, but they are delicate organisms. Imagine how a worm feels when it's hit with a dose of chemicals. It does what you'd expect—it dies. If not, the chemicals can concentrate in their bodies and kill off the birds that eat them.

What is lethal to them are copper compounds, chloropicrin, methane, sodium methyl bromide, DDT and chlordane, for example. Read the labels of anything you intend to put into your garden. Some other inorganics that can harm beneficial organisms include ammonium nitrate, ammonium phosphate, potassium nitrate and potassium chloride. These may provide nutrient salts immediately, which a plant may need. But don't count on them to help out your soil over the long term.

The natural world is very complicated and we simply haven't got enough information about it. Once we start tampering, we're just as apt to do damage. Apart from all the other dangers, chemical fertilizers are expensive. Go simple, go natural.

ABOUT NITROGEN FERTILIZERS: You're going to hear about how organic this or that fertilizer is because it's made of nitrogen. What could be more organic? Nitrogen is in the air—in fact, about 78 percent of the atmosphere is made of gaseous nitrogen. It's free, of course, but during the processing to make fertilizer, a great deal is lost and a huge amount of energy is required.

Healthy soil has enough nitrogen-fixing bacteria for any plant's requirements. These antibiotic-producing bacteria keep plant disease under control.

By using synthetics, you can end up making your plants much more vulnerable to disease. High nitrogen fertilizers can kill off some of the natural nitrogen-fixing bacteria. With soluble nitrates, remaining bacteria can then become dependent on artificial nitrogen. Once you start that, how do you stop?

Nitrates can build up in both water and plant tissues. Research from the Massachusetts Institute of Technology shows that bacteria convert nitrates to nitrites. These become the raw material for nitrosamines, which can cause cancer in animals. Run-off of nitrates into ponds and streams can cause a build-up of algae and other aquatic vegetation, which use up the oxygen supply in the water. Then the living creatures in the water are bumped off.

OTHER STUFF TO AVOID:

Potassium nitrate: 39 percent potash, 13 percent nitrogen. It separates the clay particles and long-term use will ruin the soil by destroying its porosity.

Potassium sulphate: 48 percent potash, 16 percent sulphur in the form of gypsum. It contains micronutrients that you can't control.

THE ORGANICS

The most efficient way to fertilize is to imitate nature. Soil originally came from rock. Since soils and plants evolved at the same time, using the minerals from rocks will feed them when they need the nutrients. The warmer and more moist the atmosphere, the faster nutrients will become available to the plants and the better they'll grow. And there's no problem with an excess supply that might harm plants.

ROCK FERTILIZERS: Many organic producers swear by rock powders. When you read about the extraordinary results produced by them, you realize that they are among the best of organic fertilizers. Any kind of organic matter is going to improve your soil's capacity to retain water. They will also keep nitrogen in the soil and make nutrients available to plants.

GREEN TIPS

ALL ABOUT ROCK FERTILIZERS

- Rock fertilizers provide trace elements to the soil as they break down slowly. You should apply them with organic matter since they do not supply any nitrogen. They last from 5 to 10 years.
- Phosphate rock is a source of phosphorus and trace elements including zinc, boron, iodine, iron oxide, iron

sulphide, calcium fluoride, calcium carbonate and manganese dioxide. It's not soluble in water, but stays put in
the soil so it's always available for use when the roots
finally reach it. Superphosphate is treated with sulphuric
acid. This makes it more soluble but also more expensive
because it uses so much energy in production. It's easy,
of course, and that makes it very tempting. It can cause
imbalances in soil microbes and a build-up of salts. I
used it with great abandon until I found this out.

- Granite dust is an excellent source of potash. It has trace
  elements and is a lot cheaper than chemical potash fertilizers. It won't change the pH and is slow to release. You
  can use it as a top dressing.
- Potash rock contains potassium plus a wide variety of
  trace minerals. Apply with organic material straight into
  the soil or the compost heap.

MANURES: I use composted sheep manure, which has a higher
nitrogen content than cow manure—sheep digest more efficiently than cows. Some organic gardeners don't like the idea
of using any kind of animal by-products, though this hasn't
bothered me so far. We now know, however, that the gases
produced by cows burping methane are adding to the greenhouse effect.

There is a never-ending supply of animal manure: one
cow will produce 27,000 pounds (12,250 kilograms) a year of
which only about a third is returned to the soil without being
damaged. Manure contains a high content of bacteria.

Cold manure (cow, hog manure) has a high water
content and ferments slowly.

Hot manure (sheep, poultry, horse) is richer in nitrogen
and more easily fermented. These should all be well rotted.

There are now sources for goose, chicken and mushroom manure. Check your source to see how it's produced.

Worm castings are among the most gorgeous-looking and best stuff to use on your soil. They are richer in calcium, potassium and phosphorus than any other organic product.

Rodale's *Encyclopedia of Organic Gardening* stresses that it's pointless to make comparisons between the NKP of synthetic fertilizers and manure. Manure is far more valuable: it provides trace elements not found in the synthetics, as well as organic matter necessary to the life of the soil. Organic matter turns into humus. Humus makes nutrients available to plants.

Fresh animal manure can burn plant roots. It should be well composted to make it safe and to destroy any weed seeds.

WHEN TO APPLY MANURE:

Spring: Add it as you prepare your beds. You can apply it to sod before a light rain, but not when you're expecting a heavy rain.

Summer: Side dress near plants; top dress around plants when you have put them in the soil.

Fall: Apply it after you've cleaned up the garden, prepared the beds for winter and there's been a hard frost.

Winter: Add manure to the extra leaves in plastic bags; then add a bit of soil, moisten and tie up the bags. Store in a work shed. In spring, you'll have excellent compost.

MANURE TEAS: My hort guru Juliet makes what she calls *Eau de Chickshit,* which she swears by. Like other *eaux de vie,* it must sit and ferment properly. Put chicken manure in a bucket of water. Strain and put the solid wastes into the compost and the liquid into a bottle. Measure about 5 inches (12.7 centimetres) from the edges of the lateral branches of the plant, and make a little channel with a trowel. Add the liquid to the channel. Tomatoes love this treatment. So does just about everything else.

FISH EMULSION FERTILIZER: Make your own fish emulsion: put fish scraps in a large container and add water. Cover top with wire screening to keep out animals and insects; put in an isolated location to ferment for 8 to 12 weeks. This stuff can get pretty high—add citrus oil or scent to mask some of the odour. When it's finished, a layer of mineral-rich oil will float on top of the water, and the fish scales will have sunk to bottom. Skim off the oil and store in a special container. Dilute 1 cup (250 millilitres) in 5 gallons (22 litres) of water. It's rich in nitrogen, phosphorus and trace elements, but low in calcium.

OTHER ORGANICS: Dried blood is 10 to 12 percent nitrogen. Steamed bone meal is 1 to 3 percent nitrogen, 10 to 15 percent phosphorus. Raw bone meal is richer in nitrogen—3 to 6 percent—than steamed, but it's slower to decompose.

Hoof and horn meal is 10 to 16 percent nitrogen and about 2 percent phosphorus.

If you have meat scraps and fat, or fish scraps: bury deeply to keep out of the way of animals but within reach of mature plant roots.

Also look for products based on composted manures and natural minerals in pelletized form, which condition soil and provide nutrients. These products won't burn plants and are environmentally safe.

FOLIAR FEEDING: If your soil hasn't had time to build up enough organic matter, you may need to do some short-term foliar feeding. This is feeding plants through their leaves by spraying. Use this method if there's been a heat wave or you haven't been able to water regularly. As well, use when plants are flowering or setting fruit. Spray in the morning when the plants are getting revved up for activity and it's fairly calm. Use a kelp-based product derived from marine plants.

ORGANIC FERTILIZER

PRODUCT	Approximate percentage Nitrogen (N), Phosphrus (P), Potassium (K)		
	N	P	K
Raw bone meal	2-5	14-27	0
Steamed bone meal	.7-4	18-35	0
Rock phosphate	0	20-30	0
Sulphate of potash magnesium	0	0	22
Blood meal	12	0	0
Seaweed concentrate	1	2	3
Fish emulsion	5-6	4-10	1-5

Source: The Ecological Agriculture Projects

4

BUGS

THE GOOD, THE BAD AND THE MERELY UGLY

I t took years before I admitted that other things besides
plants lived in my garden. Bugs, for one. I strolled through
my garden quite oblivious to leaves with their edges all
chewed up, foliage lacy with holes or flower buds mysteri-
ously lopped off. Until I saw my first slug. Maybe I was up
earlier than usual. Maybe I was peering under a leaf. But
there it was, slimy, oozing a sticky trail from its yucky, soft
body. Without hesitating, I picked it up and stepped on it. I
was blooded, as they say in hunting.

I got a pair of slug-stomping slippers. I started the slug
patrol and opened my eyes to all sorts of other untoward
things going on in the garden. I'd heard about earwigs, but
didn't see one until a couple of years later. Once bitten, I
started after them, too. Then came sowbugs, aphids—flying,
crawling, creeping creatures getting smaller and smaller until
I was policing the joint with a large magnifying glass.

I did not like what I saw—the more I looked, the more

insects there seemed to be out there. As I sat outside for the last breath of fresh air before bed, I imagined a throng ready to start chewing the minute I disappeared. The sound of munching sometimes haunted my sleep. I got confused— surely these living creatures can't all be bad?

Since I didn't want to spend most of my gardening time on death-squad tactics, I decided to concentrate on the worst pests and hope that my plants would survive on their own. My job, I felt, was to design the garden properly, feed and water the plants regularly and surely they'd survive without chemical warfare.

It's heartbreaking to see the evidence of our fear—no, it is hatred—of insects. Any conventional nursery shows ample evidence of this displeasure: shelves filled with rows of skulls and crossbones, warnings to keep these products away from children and other animals and to protect yourself against toxic side effects. If you have to protect yourself so carefully, how's a poor little plant going to manage?

We're not quite sure how we got ourselves into this fix, but one theory is that chemical companies developed all these herbicides and chemicals for the possibility of germ warfare. After World War II was over, there was nowhere to use them, unless the public could be convinced to buy them to get rid of everything that flew, buzzed or bit. Thus, we became addicted to the quick fix.

Quel balderdash. Almost all insects, apart from those that have no effect at all, are either beneficial to us or are essential to our well-being. Although there are 2 to 3 million species of insects, only .1 percent are pests for food crops, and even fewer will mess up the garden. Seems hardly a fair war when you look at the man-made instruments of destruction. Remember that many of the .1 percent also help to maintain the natural balance of life in your garden—earwigs, for an obvious example. There is an old garden saw that says, "If it moves slowly enough, step on it; if it doesn't, leave it— it'll probably kill something else." It's not a bad piece of advice.

To get back to pesticides for a moment—everyone should know why they are bad. One reason is that there's no such thing as a pesticide that specifically targets certain creatures, despite what you read on the bottle. It might not be toxic for some beneficials (say, bees), but it could be death for others (the utterly necessary earthworm). Dr. Stuart B. Hill says that the more you use pesticides, the more you'll need to use them. "This is because of the damage to natural controls and inevitable development of resistance and secondary pests." Most chemicals are incredibly inefficient. They usually miss the target and hit something they shouldn't, such as our own vulnerable organs and all the beneficial organisms so impor- tant to the natural mix. Keeping that mix as diversified as pos- sible is crucial to survival.

As Dr. Hill points out, there is increasing cost, decreas- ing availability and increasing dependency on something derived from non-renewable resources. "The benefits of pes- ticide use are experienced primarily by the user whereas their harmful side effects must be paid for by the population at large, including the unborn populations."

If that's not a compelling enough argument, we are acquiring more allergies because of these chemicals. Since most of them are sprayed, they become wind-borne and cover a much larger area than you had any idea you were attack- ing. They can hang about long after their toxic properties are useful. Who knows how and what beings are affected? In other words, we're losing control of our environment when we use these chemicals. If you believe you can control nature, there is no limit to the assault and damage you can perpetrate on something so very complex.

Many of the chemicals used in pesticides were developed for chemical warfare. Stuff like malathion and diazinon (lethal to honeybees) freezes nerves and muscles. If you use any of these, you have to wear protective clothing. Parathion can be absorbed by the skin. These chemicals can kill just about anything else as well as what they're supposed to be hitting.

Though some organophosphates break down into nontoxics sooner than other chemicals, the newer pesticides—the neonicotinoids—are modelled on nicotine: they excite the nerves, eventually leading to paralysis and death. Germany banned them in 2008 because they kill bees. Think of the mass die-off of bees that has been going on for the past few years. One of the many reasons for these deaths has to be the vast numbers of chemicals we float around in.

As well, we do not know how insects are going to react to the increasingly confused climate conditions. Some bugs may be on the move to new areas, where they may be deemed good or bad; only the future will tell us this. So stop thinking about insects as pests; put them in perspective. They are, after all, part of the ecosystem you've created in your garden. Perhaps you are the problem and not some poor bug. Maybe you've introduced some imbalance to the garden that draws them inexorably. It's pretty hard to manage or control creatures we don't know much about and who elude us with their mystery.

In these times of changing climate, we have no idea where insects are heading. Just look at the mountain pine beetle voraciously chewing its way through western forests, moving over the Rockies and heading for the great boreal forest where masses of vulnerable jack pines are waiting. We have no idea how to stop this, but you can bet that if we start messing around, we'll probably make it worse.

In the garden at least we have some control over nature. If you choose strong, healthy plants, put them in the right place and feed and water the soil properly, the amount of damage any pest can do is often minimal. By interplanting flowers and vegetables, by companion planting, by growing a wide diversity of plants, you will help your garden stay healthy. This is the preventative approach to gardening.

You will be hearing more and more about sustainable agriculture or permaculture (permanent agriculture). These terms are redefining our approach to the land, encouraging us to see it not merely in terms of the tonnes of crops we produce or the dollars we receive, but as part of a whole. We may have to relearn the natural systems and how they function. We must learn to imitate nature. It's not a them versus us situation with bugs and diseases. If we change the way we approach pests in the garden, this will, in the long run, encourage change in the way society sees agriculture. Organic farming has made huge strides into being accepted as mainstream—just note the number of organic farmers' markets everywhere. And short-term gain is not part of this system.

So don't look for the quick fix. Take the time to find out what role bugs have in the natural system. If you give the soil what it needs and if you practise balanced fertilization (as in lots of composting), you'll eliminate many of your garden problems. Bugs can be informative. They're there for a reason. So instead of going on a rampage with spray can in hand, take what Eliot Coleman calls the cause-correction approach—be participatory rather than antagonistic. He calls it biological diplomacy. I call it preventative gardening—making the connections between your healthy soil, the right plants and the life cycles of insects. This may be a bit more complex than you've been used to since it means not planting in the pesty period of a bug's life cycle. You need to do your research to know what might affect a plant and when.

I've tried just about every alternative form of pest control that I could find. Most have provided middling success. But the best, most effective way to deal with any kind of pest, I'm here to report, is the most conservative way possible: hand-picking. No quick fixes in that. Know your enemy. Be able to identify them, be aware of their habits. For instance, I've had a real hate on for earwigs, but earwigs also eat aphid eggs and other spoilers so I stopped trying to get rid of all of them. They, too, have a proper place in the garden. I swear that since I came to this conclusion, there are fewer around. Or I just don't notice them any more. I certainly haven't been bitten by one recently.

I still follow well-entrenched habits: armed with a flash-light, I pick slugs up after twilight falls or in the first light of dawn. Call me sick but it gives me great pleasure to pick the slimy little devils off plants and squish them underfoot. Slug patrol. I don't mind the goo on my hands and I've learned a lot about slugs in the process. One is that they move faster than you might suspect; two, they can dive down deep into the earth; and three, it must be incredibly cruel to throw them in a dish of salt to dry them right out. They writhe and, I imagine, anthropomorphically, scream in sluggy agony. Not that I'm sentimental about slugs, but it's faster grinding them under your heel anyway.

The not-so-conventional wisdom is that insect pests are symptoms of something else wrong in the garden. Perhaps there's something lacking in the soil, or in the way you planted or organized your garden. Look in that direction first. Remember the organic mantra: treat the soil, not the plant. I have a healthy garden and I also have a lot of slugs. It depends on the weather. I also get leafminer on my columbine, mildew on some of the phlox. So I stomp on the slugs, cut the leaves off anything that looks like it has leafminer and move the phlox to places with better air circulation.

GREEN TIPS
SIMPLE STEPS TO PEST CONTROL

Learn as much as you can about your plants, build up a healthy soil and follow these rules:

- Pick off pests by hand.
- Create barriers with ashes or diatomaceous earth so pests can't get at the plant.
- Add companion plants to repel the pests.
- Mix a solution of soap and water in a spray bottle and deliver a direct blast to the offender.
- Attract birds and beneficial bugs by planting what they like.
- If you are desperate, use one of the ecological pest controls listed below.

ECOLOGICAL PESTICIDES

We are certainly hearing more and more about ecological pesticides since it's now recognized that there is a buck to be made in going green. As the chemical companies do their best to green up, you'll be seeing the "organic" label on a lot of products. Be wary. For instance, fish emulsion and botanical powders do have some synthetic ingredients such as stabilizers. Botanical pesticides, derived from plants instead of chemicals, aren't necessarily safer but they break down rapidly and the effects are short-lived. They tend to disrupt natural systems less violently, but some have a few problems of their own. For instance, cyanide is produced by clover, but that doesn't mean it's good for anyone's health.

BACILLUS THURIGIENSIS (Bt): Bt is a natural bacterium that kills such caterpillar pests as cabbageworm, gypsy moth larvae and corn borer. It's generally considered to be about the best material you can use and is relatively benign. But, but, but—there are different strains for different species, so check the label.

DIATOMACEOUS EARTH: Derived from the shells of one-celled plants called diatoms, which lived millions of years ago, the fossilized remains are a fine chalk-like rock. (It's sometimes used to filter wine.) But diatomaceous earth has high levels of free silica. This can damage lungs, causing silicosis, so you must protect yourself when using it. Basalt dust does the same job and is safer. Both have microscopic needles that scratch the waterproof covering of insects' bodies, dehydrating them.

ROTENONE, RYANIA, SABADILLA AND PYRETHRUM: You should be cautious about using these organic products. They break down quickly enough but can be toxic to some beneficial bugs, fish and humans if handled improperly. I usually avoid them.

POLITICALLY CORRECT SUPPLIES

- Insecticidal soap is your first line of defence in the war against pests. You have to have a keen eye to make a direct hit on the bug. You can also bathe leaves in the soap. It won't hurt ladybugs (ladybirds) and other beneficials. There are brand-name products, but why bother when you can make your own so easily (see below)?
- There are better horticultural oils now available—much lighter and less lethal than in the past. Check the labels

to make sure they aren't out-of-date. Newer oils can be applied even when temperatures drop below 40°F (7°C), but they are not recommended above 90°F (32°C).

• Tanglefoot is still available and can be applied around trees to ward off caterpillars, ants and other ambulatory insects. It will also attract bees, though, so be careful when you put it out.

• Live nematodes attack 230 species of soil and boring insects—cutworms, grubs, weevils, gypsy moth larvae. You know when these insects are in your soil because the big predators (raccoons or skunks) will be digging in the dirt. Live nematodes are most helpful. Read the instructions very carefully as they have to be applied at the right time of the year. They will usually last 3 or 4 years.

• Biocontrol agents such as trichogramma (tiny parasitic wasps) and ladybirds can be purchased and they are very effective. However, if they are imported from great distances, they are likely to move away quickly.

NON-COMMERCIAL ALTERNATIVES

I like these homemade products better than anything in a spray can. Even if the product is environmentally friendly, its container is still unrecyclable garbage. No matter which kind you use, commercial or homemade, don't embark on a spray program during the blossom season or on any day that is not cool and still. Spray in the evening to avoid bees. You sure don't want to hit any of them.

The most effective general spray is to mix 1 teaspoon (5 millilitres) of Ivory soap (or anything pure—no detergents, which will burn) into a pint (1/2 litre) of water. It's good to have this on hand at all times.

HOMEMADE SOLUTIONS FOR PEST PROBLEMS:

- **Asparagus juice:** Spray on tomato leaves to protect them from bad nematodes.

- **Garlic and horseradish extracts, and tannic acid:** These are good repellents and may prevent insects from eating plants, but these are only temporary solutions.

- **Garlic spray:** Soak 3 to 4 chopped garlic cloves in 2 tablespoons (15 millilitres) mineral oil for a day; add a pint (1/2 litre) of water; stir, strain; a dilute 1:20 water solution of this will zap most pests.

- **Garlic and onion spray:** Add a small chopped onion to the garlic spray recipe to make an effective general spray.

- **Hot pepper:** Grind up two to four hot peppers with one small onion, a bulb of garlic and 1 quart (1 litre) water; leave for a day, then strain. Add enough water to make a gallon (4 litres). Bury the mash. A direct hit will dispatch ants, cabbageworms, spiders and caterpillars. Dried ground-up hot pepper dusted on tomato plants and cayenne pepper dusted on plants wet with dew are both excellent against a caterpillar infestation.

- **Pyrethrum:** Crush pyrethrum flowers in a blender with water; strain and use as a spray for aphids. This material is in many commercial blends and is considered a beneficial botanical.

- **Soap:** Mix 2 teaspoons (10 millilitres) Ivory with a gallon (4 litres) of warm water plus 1 tablespoon (15 millilitres) vegetable oil.

- **Sugar:** Apply 5 pounds (2.2 kilograms) to 100 pounds (45 kilograms) of soil. This will kill nematodes in 24 hours.

- **Sumac:** Chop up sumac leaves and bury sacks of them around apple trees infested with woolly aphids.

- **Tansy:** Mix 1 ounce of tansy (30 grams) with 1¼ cup (310 millilitres) water. Process in a blender or food processor. Strain and spray.
- **Tomato:** Chop up tomato leaves, soak in water, then strain. Or boil stems and leaves in water; cool, strain. Spray on roses to destroy black or green flies, caterpillars and aphids. You could even try freezing the mixture over the winter to have it ready for the new season, though I haven't done this myself.
- **Wormwood:** Make a tea to spray on the ground in fall and spring to discourage slugs; spray on fruit trees to repel aphids.

A GARDEN FOR BENEFICIALS

A garden to attract the good bugs, or beneficials, will include mulch for ladybirds, sugar for lacewings, ground cover for spiders and ground beetles and a patch of aromatic herbs for bees and hover flies. Remember that hybrid flowers won't attract bees, wasps or hover flies. They like bright-coloured flowers of different sizes, blossom shapes and fragrance—see the list of plants for pollinators below. Be sure to have a place for these bugs to drink. Allow water to sit long enough—at least an hour—to let chemicals such as chlorine evaporate before setting it out for these friends. Other methods of attracting beneficials:

- Plant your garden with sunflowers, small shrubs (roses, elder, blackberries) and trees. This will attract ladybugs and provide the right kind of habitat.
- Plant a strip of the following flowers: bee balm, comfrey, rudbeckia, butterfly bush. This mix will attract tachinid and syrphid flies.

- The Canadian Organic Growers' magazine recommends planting a row of sunflowers and kochias. The latter is a 5-foot (150-centimetre) annual with red, green or yellow leaves that reseeds and provides an insect barrier. (It is also considered a noxious weed in some areas, so check before using.) They also recommend stacking the fibrous stalks of vegetables against this in the fall to attract lady-bugs, which, in turn, will eat the bugs emerging from the stalks. Everything can be composted in spring.
- Have a strip of grass running through your garden. Fill it with the right kind of weeds to attract beneficials: Queen-Anne's lace, dandelions, clover.
- Bits of raised wood placed judiciously about will encourage spiders, ground beetles and praying mantises to come in to rest or to deposit eggs. These creatures eat anything.
- Trap plants such as nasturtiums will attract aphids.
- **Plants for pollinators:** columbine (*Aquilegia canadensis*); serviceberry (*Amelanchier* spp.); *Anemone* spp.; dogwood (*Cornus* spp.); ninebark (*Physocarpus opulifolius*); elder (*Sambucus* spp.); hyssop (*Agastache* spp.); swamp milk-weed (*Asclepias incarnata*); butterfly weed (*A. tuberosa*); New England aster (*Symphyotrichum novae-angliae*); Joe-Pye weed (*Eupatorium* spp.); sunflowers (*Helianthus* spp.); cardinal flower (*Lobelia cardinalis*); bergamot, bee balm (*Monarda* spp.); coneflower (*Rudbeckia* spp.); purple coneflower (*Echinacea* spp.) and, of course, goldenrod (*Solidago* spp.). (Note that spp. after the botanical name of a plant means that there are many different species.)

In addition to beneficials, you also want to attract bats, birds, frogs and toads. They're excellent, all-natural pest controllers and they work for free.

Bats: Bats are prodigious eaters of insects. They can consume up to 5,000 insects every night. This includes grasshoppers, corn borers and cutworm moths. Don't worry about their droppings. They are no worse than most birds. We have lots of bats looping around our house and trees at night (a fact my kids kept secret for years) and I've never seen anything that even looks vaguely like bat guano. If you don't have the right habitat, put up a bat house to attract them to your garden. Since they are nocturnal, they aren't going to bother you much and they will keep your space free of mosquitoes.

Birds: Birds eat grubs, beetles and flying insects. You can buy bird feed but make sure you have the right mix and only buy it from a reputable bird store. You don't want exotic stuff in there for your local songbirds. There isn't just one good fix even when it comes to bird food. Get one of these dandy bird-feeding stations that will close up shop when something heavier than a small bird lands on it—something pesky like a squirrel.

Almost any plant with red blossoms will attract birds. A birdbath will draw them as well as provide water for the good bugs. But the water should be changed every day to remove the possibility of mosquito larvae developing and because fresh water is best for birds.

A wild section of trees and shrubs will keep useful woodpeckers, chickadees and nuthatches in residence. If you leave animal hair, string and rags strategically placed, the birds will have nesting materials. And plant trees with exfoliating bark such as *Stewartia pseudocamellia,* paperback maple (*Acer griseum*) and especially seven-son flower (*Heptacodium miconoides*) so the birds can tear strips off them for building nests.

Frogs and toads: If you can safely attract them to your garden, they will each eat up to 10,000 insects in three months. They consume grubs, cutworms, sowbugs, moths, flies and chinch bugs. Frogs will be more likely to hang about a pond. Toads are ground lovers and will need protection from the sun and from cats. Provide shelter in the winter. Toad houses are enchanting.

GOOD BUGS

Assassin bugs: They have a long proboscis, which they use to inject lethal saliva into prey. They eat caterpillars, Japanese beetles and leafhoppers.

Bees: Bees are essential to life. Bumblebees are native (unlike the honeybee, which is an introduced species). They pollinate plants, allowing them to bear fruit. No pollination, no plant life. They can see blue and yellow flowers but not red (though this doesn't stop them from going to red plants such as bee balm, which got its name for a good reason). They love the yellow-centred blossoms of fruit trees, raspberries, strawberries (which also provide nesting sites for stem-nesting bees) and members of the Umbelliferae (Apiaceae) family, which includes fennel and parsnip. Never spray dormant oil when the trees are blooming or you'll wipe out the bees.

Other plants to consider: Joe-Pye weed, sweetpea, Russian sage, lavender and other herbs, salvias, asters, old favourites such as forsythia and pussy willow and annuals such as cosmos and cleome. Bumblebees are wonderful to observe because they do bumble around. As well, they can work with less light than honeybees, so their days are longer.

Braconid wasps: These tiny wasps will parasitize larvae of gypsy moths, codling moth, tent caterpillars, cutworms, strawberry leafroller and oriental fruit moth. In areas where pesticides haven't been used, they can get rid of the destruc tive gypsy moth. The female injects her eggs into a caterpillar; the larvae hatch, feed inside the body and then chew their way out. Plant fennel, parsley, Queen-Anne's lace, clover and yarrow to attract them.

Big-eyed bugs: A big-eyed bug nymph can eat as many as 1,600 spider mites before it becomes an adult (when it slows down and eats 80 a day). They feed on aphids, leafhoppers and whiteflies. Plant goldenrod to attract them.

Chalcid wasps: They are parasitoids and will devour mealybugs, aphids, scale and the larvae of moths, beetles and butterflies. You can buy these commercially and release them into your garden.

Damselflies: Damselflies eat aphids, leafhoppers, treehoppers and small caterpillars.

Encarsia wasps: These are parasitic to whiteflies.

Ichneumon wasps: They can clean up the spruce sawfly, wood-boring caterpillars and tomato moth. They are tireless in cleaning up aphids.

Fireflies or lightning bugs: They live in low vegetation and feed on slugs and snails.

Ground beetles: There are many species, some are brown, others bright green.

Ground beetle: This species is black with a slight iridescence; it lives in the soil and eats a variety of plant pests.

Raised beds will attract these fierce-looking beetles. I was terrified of them until I found out that they were A Good Thing. They are big and black with a slight iridescence—a shiny, dark green tinge on the thorax—and purple elsewhere. Leave them alone. They are not to be confused with June beetles, which are less rounded and much bigger. Ground beetles are nocturnal; they live in soil and under rocks and logs during the day, so make sure they have shelter and water. They eat loads of slugs, and go after gypsy moth larvae, cankerworms, armyworms and cutworms. Be careful, they can pinch fiercely.

Hover flies: Hover flies look like wasps, and they do hover. They don't sting and have tiny antennae and a flattened abdomen, unlike a wasp, which has long antennae and a cylindrical abdomen. They are also pollinators. Plants to attract them include baby blue eyes, cosmos, marigold, meadow foam, spearmint and all members of the daisy family.

Lacewings: They are attracted to all members of the carrot family: Queen-Anne's lace, wild lettuce or oleander, red cosmos, angelica, goldenrod and tansy. The larvae are called aphid lions because they have such a voracious appetite for these bugs. Each egg is laid on a separate long, silky stalk to keep them from eating their siblings. A light will draw these nocturnally active creatures. They also consume spider mites, leafhoppers, thrips, moth eggs, red mites and caterpillars.

Lacewing: A beneficial bug. It is active at night, and eats many small insect pests.

Ladybirds (ladybugs): They are probably everyone's favourite bug. The larvae can munch 25 aphids an hour. And one coupling will produce from 200 to 1,000 offspring. They can get into areas no spray could possibly penetrate. Plant angelica, butterfly weed, nasturtium, marigold, tansy, evergreen euonymus, goldenrod, morning glory and yarrow to attract them to your garden. If you buy ladybugs, try to get those raised locally—ones raised far away won't stay in your garden. Unless you've got the right habitat, ladybugs go into decline, or they'll leave your garden for one that suits them better. Unfortunately, most of the native species have been displaced recently by foreign species. Remember the great Asian ladybug invasion of a few years ago? They came in on plants and multiplied to plague proportions.

Parasitic wasps: Trichogramma are parasitic wasps that destroy the eggs of many moths, butterflies and loopers (moth caterpillars). They appreciate a wildflower assortment—any nectar-producing flowers with an open single flower, members of the carrot and daisy family, buttercup, goldenrod, strawberries and white clover.

Praying mantis: They like clumps of goldenrod, cosmos, raspberries and other brambles. They look a bit like grasshoppers with strong front legs—hence the praying position they seem to take. Dormant from the beginning of November to middle of May, they can clean up your garden during the growing season although they might also eat some of the beneficials. Eggs are laid in fall, hatch in May and June, mature through the summer and die in fall. In sequence, first they eat aphids, then leafhoppers and, in adulthood, chinch bugs, crickets, caterpillars and leafhoppers. They also feed on mosquitoes and flies, and they eat moths at night.

Praying mantis: A useful bug, often found in clumps of brambles, it attacks and eats a wide variety of insects.

Rove beetle: There are hundreds of different species of rove beetles. They have very short wing covers (elytra), a long dark, flat body a bit like an earwig but without the curved appendages at the stern. They eat red spiders, cabbage maggots and larvae of cabbage fly.

Syrphid flies: Also known as flower flies, they are aphid predators as larvae but the adults, which look like wasps, feed on pollen and nectar. If your rose bush is infested with aphids, syrphid flies will find the pests and wipe them out in a few days (eating an aphid a minute). In addition, they love leafhoppers, mealybugs, spiders, mites and scale. Any member of the daisy family will attract them.

Tachinid flies: They look like houseflies and they muck about around flowers drinking up nectar. Some fill their caterpillar hosts with maggots. They can destroy larvae of gypsy moths, sawflies, cutworms, armyworms and Mexican bean beetles. Wild buckwheat attracts them.

Yellowjackets: They are considered beneficial—unless you happen to be allergic to their stings. They feed on caterpillars and harmful flies. If they start being a pain in the neck when you are eating outside, leave a little bit of meat or something sugary over to one side of the table to lure them away from your food.

Herbs for beneficials: Anise, caraway, catnip, coriander, cumin, dill, fennel, lavender, sweet marjoram, mint, rosemary, autumn and pineapple sage, winter savoury, tansy and thyme.

Flowers for beneficials: Every native plant will attract beneficials, as will any simple flower that hasn't been hybridized.

BAD BUGS

These insects are the ones that irritate us the most because they nibble away at leaves, mess up the lawn and generally misbehave—at least by human standards. One of the simplest ways of dealing with them, apart from handpicking or direct sprays of water, is to install trap crops. These will attract the nuisances away from other plants to the trap crop. *Voilà!* You've got them all in one place. So when you hear that nasturtiums are a pain to grow because they get covered with aphids, it's not quite true. The nasturtiums are seducing the pests away from all the other plants in the area, making it easier for you to catch them *en masse*. You can be sure, however, that if you do get an infestation, predators will move in pretty quickly. The reason: they can get a lot more protein from a bug than a mere plant.

GREEN TIPS
GENERAL PEST PREVENTION

- Good drainage is essential for controlling pests. Don't leave wet stuff around for long.
- Clean up dead leaves and debris around plants.
- Give your plants good hosing down if you do notice some tiny blighter on the attack.
- A general rule for flying insects is to make your own controls. At one time I recommended using sticky yellow disks covered with Tanglefoot paste (it's a balsam resin) to attract them. But this also attracts and traps bees, which are attracted to yellow. So unless you've got a really bad infestation, rethink this strategy.

Ants: Not all ants are bad; they destroy larvae of houseflies and fruit flies. I love watching the stroking motions of ants as they sip on the sap of buds. It won't hurt the plant, so leave them alone. Ants also help aerate the soil. However, ants look after aphids and planthoppers and protect them against their enemies, the beneficials. So if you are overrun, try the following:

- Sage, lavender, southernwood and hyssop will keep them away.
- If they are infesting your roses, make a tea of ferns and pour it around the affected plants.

- Strawberries attract ants—make a tea of southernwood and, when the tea is cool, pour over the plants.
- Plant pennyroyal (a creeping mint), spearmint or tansy near the kitchen to keep them away.
- For a bad infestation, blend orange peels with a little orange juice to make a thick paste and pour it over the ant hills.

Black ants: If black ants are invading the house, put 1 teaspoon (5 millilitres) rotenone, 1 teaspoon (5 millilitres) honey, and 1 teaspoon (5 millilitres) water in an old lid. Place in the cupboard or any area ants seem to be congregating.

Carpenter ants: They have a bad reputation as chewers of wood, but what they really indicate is that you have a problem—*they* are not the problem. They nest where wood has already disintegrated. Plant aromatic tansy by all doors. Diatomaceous earth sprinkled along their path will dry them out. When it's mixed with honey, they will take it back to the nest and that way may kill the queen.

Fire ants: Pour 1 tablespoon (15 millilitres) borax on the ant hill to keep them in check. Make a manure tea and pour it over the hill; mix 2 teaspoons (10 millilitres) borax in a pint (1/2 litre) of apple jelly and drop the sticky stuff around the mound—workers will carry it to the queen and it will kill her.

Aphids: Beneficials that eat aphids include ladybird beetles, green lacewings, syrphid flies, hover flies and parasitic wasps. Trap plants such as nasturtiums, plantain and lamb's-quarters will draw aphids away from other plants. Chives, garlic, pennyroyal, southernwood, nasturtium, coriander, tansy and anise act as repellents.

Aphid: Nearly every species of plant is adversely affected by some species of this tiny pest.

Most types of aphids can overwinter. They are tiny and produce up to twenty generations a year. They are visible on leaves and shoots. Look for gall-like swellings on leaves; another sign is curling, sometimes yellow, leaves. By sucking the sap, aphids cause foliage to wither. They produce a honeydew that is exuded from the anus. This gets all over the surface of leaves and shoots, turns them sticky and blots out light. This in turn produces black mould, which blocks out even more sun. The disease is carried from plant to plant by the winged form of aphids. Ants herd aphids to keep them together for the honeydew, so ant activity is one way you can spot an aphid problem.

GREEN TIPS
DEALING WITH APHIDS

- Don't leave discarded plants around. Thoroughly cultivate areas where you've had to remove plants.
- Aphids may indicate low nitrogen content in your soil.
- Dust the undersides of leaves with baking powder.
- If aphids infect apple, quince or pear, use one of the new dormant-oil sprays in spring (not during the blossom season, of course).
- If you've got aphids on your rose bushes, sprinkle a soap and water mixture on the insects. Use your hands to rub them off, then hose the plant down.
- Plant garlic beside your rose bushes to keep down aphids. Do this with your houseplants as well.
- Be sure to check under the leaves if you have these little devils—that's where they lay their eggs. And where they overwinter very successfully.
- Clean off the infected plant with a hose or spray with insecticidal soap. Then brush diatomaceous earth on the leaves.

- Make your own aphid traps—use a yellow dish (the animal likes yellow) and fill it with soapy water.
- Mince shallots in a food processor and make a spray. Do the same with rhubarb leaves—boil half an hour in 3 quarts (3 litres) water, add 1 quart (1 litre) water when cool. Dissolve one ounce (30 grams) soap flakes in the mix—this will help it adhere to the plant. You can make a substitute with elder leaves (this will also discourage mildew on roses).
- Spray with a strong solution of limewater.
- Take tomato leaves and chop, add 1 quart (1 litre) of boiling water, and steep. Strain. Dilute with water 4:1, and spray.
- To discourage winged aphids, put sheets of aluminum foil around plants—the reflection of the sky will confuse them.
- Grind up hot pepper and mix with black pepper. Cut with water and spray every 3 days directly on the aphids.

Chinch bugs: These are a real pain in eastern North America. They hibernate in grass. The damage to lawns is caused by the young, which are 1/5- to 1/4-inch (5- to 6- millimetres) long and reddish in colour. The adults are black with a white spot between the wings on the back. Yellowing grass, then dead patches, will tip you off. Or you'll smell them when you walk across the lawn. Another test is to cut out the ends of a large can and push it into the soil. Fill with water and any chinch bugs in the soil will float to the surface. They have a natural predator in the big-eyed bug. You will have to remove the infected areas and then reseed.

Colorado potato beetle: These insects are 1/3-inch (8 millimetres) long with a hard, convex, brownish red shell and yellow stripes. The eggs are yellow-orange and can be found on the undersides of potato leaves, as well as eggplants, peppers and tomatoes. Handpick the eggs (they can lay as many as 800 at a go), larvae and adult beetles. Another alternative is to knock them into a container of water with a little detergent added—these pests are resistant to more chemicals than any other pest. Ground beetles are a natural predator, so try to encourage this beneficial bug.

Colorado potato beetle: it is a pest of not only potato plants but also eggplants, peppers, and tomatoes.

BATTLE PLAN AGAINST POTATO BEETLES

- Interplant affected areas with garlic or marigolds.
- Squish the cluster of jelly-like orange eggs between your fingers. Or partially fill a pail with water and 1 tablespoon (15 millilitres) cooking oil. Put under the plant and gently shake the beetles into the bucket.
- Make your own bug juice of larvae and beetles blended with water and spray the leaves. Disgusting but a deterrent.
- Dust with rotenone or diatomaceous earth (the usual rule applies—wear protective clothing).
- *Bacillus thuringiensis* (Bt) will attack the larvae, but make sure it's the beetle-killing strain.

Cutworms: These are the caterpillars of the night-flying moth. They are grey-brown, 1 inch (2.5 centimetres) long and will curl up if disturbed or feeding (they love to curl around the stem of new tomato plants). Cutworms overwinter as young larvae.

You can tell they are lurking about when you see the tops of young plants lopped off or the plants are cut down at the base. In either case, cultivate deeply around the plant to expose cutworms to predators. Beneficials that feed on cutworms include trichogramma wasps, fireflies, tachinid flies and ground beetles.

GREEN TIPS
CUTTING BACK CUTWORM DAMAGE

- Protect new plants by putting toothpicks on either side of the stem.
- Tansy will repel them; a row of sunflowers around the bed will act as a trap crop.
- Use collars of paper or cardboard, or circles of onions around young transplants.
- Use oak-leaf mulch along garden paths.
- Pick them off plants at night.
- Put bran meal around transplants or try a mix of sawdust and bran with enough molasses to make a sticky goo. When cutworms climb off the plant, they are trapped in the muck.
- Circle plants with wood ashes from the fireplace.
- Spray *Bacillus thuringiensis* (Bt) around transplants.

Earwigs: These reddish brown insects with their pincer-shaped claws on the abdomen are mean. They bite. They lay their white eggs deep in the soil and overwinter in this state. You'll notice their presence by holes in flowers and foliage. Earwigs are nocturnal creatures and they like to find a dark, moist place to sleep in during the day. If you have a large infestation, be careful with your mulching. Mulch provides the perfect resting spot but it's also a good place to catch them. Beneficial bugs that destroy earwigs include tachinid flies and syrphid flies.

Earwig: Both adults and young are nocturnal, and feed on worms, small insects and young plants.

GREEN TIPS

TRAPPING AND REPELLING EARWIGS

- Don't try to get rid of all earwigs from your garden; they eat aphids and other little sucking insects. However, they also eat fresh new leaves, especially cotyledons—the first two leaves of a new plant.
- For traps, use an old pipe, garden hose, rolled-up umbrella or rolled-up corrugated cardboard left out during the day to attract them. Then dunk them into a pail of water (coat the sides of the pail with a bit of salt or soap so they can't escape).
- Half bury a small container of beer. They will fall in and die boozing.
- Leave a bucket of soapy water in the garden. Often they'll crawl in and drown.
- If they happen to get into the house—in my experience, they love to lie between sheets at the cottage—use diatomaceous earth. Put a small container of it inside a cupboard or under the sink. Sprinkle around cracks.

Grasshoppers: *Nosema locustae,* a protozoan parasite, attacks grasshoppers and some species of crickets. Dissolve in water, add bran and put around the garden. They eat it and, before they die, they pass the disease on to the next generation.

Japanese beetle: This blue, iridescent beetle can be treated with milky spore disease (*Bacillus popillae*), which can be bought in a powder dispenser. It attacks the larvae. You can also make a trap using geranium oil. Plant African marigolds and evening primrose to repel Japanese beetles. Or poison them with castor bean plant leaves or blossoms of white geraniums.

Leafminers: You can tell that these little devils are infecting your plants when white or brown tunnels or blotches appear on the leaves. I get them on my columbines. It would be nice to stop them before they do this damage, but it's the larvae that do the tunnelling and by the time you see little black flies with yellow stripes, it's too late. They emerge in spring and lay eggs throughout the summer. They may carry diseases with them.

Robins, purple finches and chickadees love leafminers. Encourage them with a birdbath or some other source of water. Trap plants for leafminers include radishes and lamb's-quarters. Plant about 15 feet (5 metres) away from an infected border. Keep picking away at them by scratching off the eggs (they are hatched when leaves develop grey blisters).

GREEN TIPS
LEAFMINER CONTROL

- Cut off any blistered leaves and get rid of them. Leave enough healthy tissue so that the plant isn't harmed.
- Handpicking is best: turn leaves of vulnerable plants over and look for chalky white eggs.

Mealybugs: There are short- and long-tail versions of these pests. They appear as clusters of white, waxy fluff on stems and on bottom leaves. Clean off leaves by a direct hit with the hose, or use an insecticidal soap or any soap and water concoction. Beneficial bugs that control mealybugs include chalcid wasps, cryptolaemus beetle and lacewing larvae. To remove mealybugs from houseplants, use a watercolor brush dipped in rubbing alcohol.

Nematodes: Also known as roundworms or eelworms, nematodes are micro-organisms that look like tiny worms. Most of the 500,000 species of nematode are useful but some of them can be lethal, sucking sap and injecting toxins into plants. Signs of nematodes include malformation of leaves, flowers, stems, dieback and yellow foliage. If you think that it's nematodes plaguing your plants, have the soil tested by a specialist (get names from your local agriculture station). Take enough samples during a time of plant growth to make at least half a pint (1/4 litre).

GREEN TIPS
NEGATING NEMATODES

- If you have a very small garden, you can sterilize the soil by lifting the soil into containers and pouring boiling water over it.
- Plant marigolds, which produce a chemical that bumps off nematodes. Let the plants decay in the soil. Rotate marigolds with other plants from year to year. If you loathe marigolds, just snip off the flowers. This, by the way, is not a quick fix, and it might take a couple of years to inoculate the soil.
- Mustard plants, roots of asparagus and hairy indigo are all good cover crops to discourage nematodes.
- Smartweed, wild chicory and chrysanthemums such as feverfew and painted daisy will also help.
- Use castor beans as a trap plant.

- Mulch with pine leaves.
- Fish emulsion repels nematodes. Use a foliar spray.
- Don't be upset by the occasional appearance of a yellow and curling leaf. Just keep on treating the soil with a good compost of leaf mould and kelp.

Slugs: You're always reading in magazines and organic publications about how to get rid of slugs and earwigs—just put out a board and collect them in the morning. Well, my garden won't hold a lot of boards. What I find most effective, especially given the way I garden, is to leave a small pile of garden detritus, preferably a little on the moist side, overnight. In the early morning, I lift the pile and stomp on any little creatures I find.

It's the little ones that do the most damage, so don't be fooled by size. They live in damp sheltered places the year round, resting during the day and coming out to dine at night.

I once read that slugs can be eliminated in three years by assiduous handpicking. You have to do this every day and keep a pretty clean garden. You can use this in conjunction with other methods, of course.

One old book recommends making a "dead line" of salt—they can't go past it and survive. Salt, of course, is sure death for slugs because it dries out their slimy little bodies.

GREEN TIPS

SLUGGING IT OUT

- To make a slug trap, slice up potatoes, carrots, cabbage or lettuce leaves for them to feed on and they might leave other plants alone. Then get after them with your stomping slippers.
- The following beneficials eat slugs: larvae of lightning

bugs, garter snakes, rove and ground beetles, ducks, box turtles and salamanders.

- One gardener I know uses a stick with a 12-inch (30-centimetre) needle-sharp spike on the end—slug shish-kebab. To keep slugs away from her beans, she secures a tall metal pole (an old pipe will do) and tops it with a hubcap into which she's drilled a dozen holes around the perimeter. She runs string from the hub-cap holes down to tent pegs on the ground, and puts slug bait all around. She gets slug-free scarlet runners.

- Slugs live in mulch. Use diatomaceous earth, ashes or something sharp and pointed around plants. If the slugs persist, handpick faithfully every day.

- When things cool off in the fall, slugs will search for protection (boards, large leaves, garden debris) and this is the time to make a great haul.

- Be sure to mulch around plants *after* the ground is frozen and after you've cleaned up around the plants.

- Use protective borders of sand, ashes, lime or metal barriers around plants—though this only works if slugs are outside the border trying to get in.

- Slugs don't like oak leaves or wood shavings.

- Hellebores keep slugs from grape vines, so plant one near the other.

- The traditional beer mix draws them out of their lairs. Put a yogurt or margarine container in a shallow hole so that it's even with the ground. Pour in beer and a little water. Partially cover to keep rain out. If the slugs tend to leave after drinking, add a little flour to make the mixture sticky.

- Here's a variation from Rodale's *Encyclopedia of Organic Gardening*: To a 2-cup (500-millilitre) plastic container almost full of water, add 1 tablespoon (15 millilitres) brewer's yeast, 1 tablespoon (15 millilitres) molasses or honey, 1 tablespoon (15 millilitres) cooking oil. This mixture will keep both slugs and earwigs from escaping. Once they're all dead, put them in the compost.

- Copper wire and crushed eggshells strewn around plants will deter slugs to some degree but remember that they will still be able to go underground.
- Make collars of window screen to keep them away from the stems of plants.
- Try sprinkling powdered ginger around plants.

Sowbugs: These little guys look like something left over from the last ice age. They have an armour-like crust, seven pairs of legs and they perpetually gobble up decaying matter. They look like pillbugs, but behave differently: when exposed, pillbugs curl up; sowbugs run for cover. The only time you should think of them as pests is if they get into the house (which means your house is way too moist) or they are eating small new plants. Mostly they live off dead and decaying stuff. Pyrethrum will get rid of them if they're a problem. Oak-leaf mulch, wood ashes in the soil or a lime solution (1 pound/454 grams in 5 gallons/20 litres of water) will help. Sowbugs help break down materials in the compost pile, but make sure there aren't any in the compost that you spread around the garden.

Spider mites: The reddish brown spidery adults are so tiny, about the size of a grain of salt, that you'll only know you've got them when you see a fine webbing of white in leaves and stems. Leaves become mottled, turn bronze and fall prematurely. Spider mites feed on leaves, fruit and roots. They lay their eggs on the leaves or buds close to the base of the plant.

VANQUISHING SPIDER MITES

- They like an arid atmosphere. Keep plants moist and cool by misting.
- Use insecticidal soap mixed with seaweed solution and spray on the undersides of new growth regularly every 2 weeks.
- Spray directly with a jet of water.
- Mix whole-wheat flour, buttermilk and water and wash spider mites off with this goo.
- Dust sulphur on both sides of the leaves before temperatures reach 90°F (32°C).
- They are repelled by onion, garlic and chives.
- Use pyrethrum in a spray directly on mites on the underside of leaves 4 days apart; or dust sabadilla on plants after a heavy dew or shower.
- Diatomaceous earth dusted on plants also helps.
- Lacewings, ladybugs and predatory mites (which are also commercially available) will help control spider mites.
- Use one of the new superior dormant-oil sprays on fruit trees in fall. It will suffocate spider mites and keep them from wintering over.
- A 2 percent oil of coriander mixed with water solution, or 2 percent emulsion of oil of lemon grass make effective sprays.

Tent caterpillars: The yellowish brown to dark brown tent caterpillar moth with two white stripes on each wing is found on fruit trees both domestic and wild. They appear in seven- to ten-year cycles. They straddle trees with cases of eggs laid in the fall; the eggs overwinter. It's the larvae—black caterpillars with whitish stripes down the back—that do the damage. Parasitic wasps may control them in some areas. Baltimore orioles will clean them up.

GREEN TIPS

EVICTING TENT CATERPILLARS:

- In spring, get rid of the new webs by wiping with a kerosene-soaked cloth—don't light it.
- Spray caterpillars with *Bacillus thuringiensis* (Bt).
- Dust with diatomaceous earth.
- Garden writer Sonia Day used to don rybber gloves, then goes around to affected trees such as chokecherries and drown tent caterpillars in soapy water. Now she just pulls off the webbing and leaves the caterpillars exposed for the birds to eat.

MAMMAL PESTS

Any number of animals may invade your garden. I'm on an ancient raccoon path and I know that they will always be there. I've watched people put out traps and carry them off, but I worry about separating mothers and babies. Sometimes there are five babies playing in my water fountain at night. I swear it's in their genes to behave as if they have a right to stroll through my garden.

You can try to animal-proof your garden: keep all fences in good repair; patch cracks and holes in wood. You can also put electric fences around the perimeter if your garden is small enough.

Birds: To discourage pigeons, starlings and other irritating birds, place weatherproof netting over any edges they fancy perching along.

Cats: I'm a cat person and, even though I adored her, my own cat was a pain in the neck when she decided to sleep on top of a particularly favoured heath. Why this plant? I don't know. A series of small sharp sticks kept her out of most parts of the garden. It's now considered very dangerous to let cats roam. They are major killers of songbirds. If you have to let your cat out, make sure it's not during the migratory period. Birds migrate mostly at night, so that's when you **must** keep cats indoors.

Deer: They are now considered the number-one garden pest. We've encroached on their habitats, so now they are making up for it all over suburbs and country gardens everywhere.

GREEN TIPS
DETERRING DEER

- Spray plants with a solution of 6 fresh eggs to 1 gallon (4 litres) of water. Also put it around the base of trees and on grasses and shrubs along trails. Renew spray after rain.
- Protect roses by breaking a whole egg beneath the bushes—it gets smelly but is not too offensive to humans.
- Make a fence 6 to 8 feet (2 to 2.5 metres) high with a 3-foot (1-metre) wide arbour on top. Stretch chicken wire on the ground beyond the outside of the fence.
- One great gardener, Francisca Darts, used Lifebuoy soap in old pantyhose around the perimeter to keep them out. She wasn't sure why Lifebuoy worked better than other soaps, but it does.
- Bags of human hair outlining your territory will also help.
- Mark the territory with your own urine. Easiest to obtain at a party: just send the men outdoors and they will know what to do.

Dogs: If you don't own one, you may find that dogs can be a drag. I have a regular canine visitor that urinates on plants near the sidewalk (watched by the doting owner). I've taken to sprinkling cayenne pepper over the spot, which does discourage it from using the same spot over and over. I'm told that Epsom salts sprinkled at the front of a border will help. Pound small sticks a foot (30 centimetres) or so apart around an area to keep dogs from trampling through easily. It's very hard to train owners who let their dogs off-leash, but a large sign saying you've just poured poison all over the front garden can sometimes get the message across that dogs can be vandals.

Gophers: Most of the suggestions for getting rid of gophers are so cruel I cannot even begin to record them. It's better to encourage natural predators such as dogs, hawks, snakes or skunks. If the gophers are pernicious, try growing your plants in 5-gallon (20-litre) plastic buckets. Remove the bottoms and drill holes in the sides; then bury them in spring. For small plants, use berry baskets.

Groundhogs: Other than drastic measures, a really good fence is your best option. You'll have to sink it fairly far into the ground. Or try planting a separate area of the garden for these animals; they like clover and alfalfa. Keep a section around the garden mowed and they may spend their time there. Natural predators are cats, dogs and hawks.

Mice: I've never really had a problem with mice but if you do, try planting caper spurge (*Euphorbia lathyris*), which will help deter them. Be careful of all the euphorbias; they have lactic acid in their stalks and can cause dermatitis if you handle them carelessly. Borders of daffodils, narcissi, scilla and grape hyacinth will also discourage mice. Make sure that you keep areas around fruit trees free of mulch. In fact, don't mulch any places mice like to nest until after the ground is frozen solid. Use plastic tree-guard strips or aluminum foil to protect trees. Cats, snakes and owls are natural enemies of mice.

Moles: If moles are a problem, it may mean that your garden is infested with all sorts of snails, ants, bees, wasps, centipedes and grubs, which they enjoy eating. In some ways, they are really doing you a favour. However, they can destroy root systems and spread plant diseases. At freeze-up, all this life retreats deeper in the soil, and the moles follow, aerating and moving humus into the subsoil. I know one gardener who, whenever she sees a mound of dirt rising up, pokes a stick down the hole, enlarges it, then drops a couple of mothballs down there. Mothballs aren't environmentally friendly, so I don't have them around. But then I don't have moles, either.

Elder leaves have a smell that repels moles. Caper spurge, also called mole plant, is supposed to fend off moles via its root exudates, but beware, this plant seeds very vigorously. Another suggestion, dump used kitty litter into their holes.

Rabbits: If you are bothered terribly by rabbits, build an 18-inch (45-centimetre) fence around the garden, but keep in mind that they will dig under it if you've got something in there they love. Try scattering onions, blood meal, cayenne and wood ashes around plants; they may act as a deterrent.

Raccoons: Nothing, I'm convinced, will discourage them. You might try, however, putting up flimsy fences around vegetable patches. Something high enough and tottery enough so they'll fall off when they reach the top.

GREEN TIPS

TEN MORE WAYS TO DISCOURAGE RACCOONS:
- They like searching for grubs, which means that when they see freshly dug earth, they go there immediately.

- They are lazy devils. Sprinkle blood meal around; renew after a rain or watering.
- I use stones or flat rocks to protect newly planted lilies from curious claws.
- Strew hydrated lime around whatever you value most. Be sure to reapply after a rainstorm.
- If you have a pond or fountain, they'll mess about in it. Drape netting material over it at night, secured by rocks if the raccoons are a real nuisance. Otherwise, be prepared for general cleanups.
- A small electric fence switched on at night is effective, if not particularly attractive.
- Flashing lights will keep them away from the garden, as will cat pee.
- Have a can filled with stones at the ready to throw in their direction. It might scare them away for days at a time.
- Once they use an area as a toilet, they will keep on using it. Clean it up on a daily basis. I hate this.
- Never ever feed them. It is criminal to do so. They are wild animals, which means you can't get out the BB gun either.

Skunks: If a skunk turns his bottom toward you, run. I got hit and ran straight into the house. This is not advised. Build a wire mesh fence about 3 feet (1 metre) above ground and 6 inches (15 centimetres) underground. To discourage them, sprinkle cayenne pepper around the perimeter of the garden.

Squirrels: They must be going through a population explosion. They are so aggressive they'll come right into the house if I leave the screen open. A friend refers to them as tree rats.

GREEN TIPS
OUTWITTING SQUIRRELS

- Remove wood piles or heaps of debris, where they can make nests.
- Get a dog.
- If you trap, get a humane trap and check on it regularly. But don't trap in spring, when you could separate mother and babies. If you release a squirrel within its range, it will just come back. Unfortunately, as you remove them, more squirrels will move in to take their place. Either give them hand-outs in one part of the garden or plant enough stuff to share.
- Scatter blood meal all over the place after planting bulbs. It will discourage squirrels and act as a fertilizer, but must be replenished each time it rains. It will also entice dogs to dig up the bed, and can make them sick if they lick their paws.
- Plant a mothball alongside each bulb. Don't bother placing them on top of the ground; that just seems to indicate where something delicious is buried. Squirrels figured this one out in about one generation.
- You could plant bulbs and then cover the area with chicken wire, but I'd worry about getting scratched. If you are careful, however, this might work.
- When planting tulips or lilies, both of which squirrels adore, accompany them with either fritillarias or daffodils. The former smell skunky, which repels squirrels, and the latter are poisonous to them.

5

DISEASES AND DEFICIENCIES

✻

When you look through gardening books from the 1940s and 1950s, you wonder how we have survived environmentally at all. It's not surprising that gardeners have a terrible reputation as serious polluters who pour toxic chemicals all over their plants. We're still stuck with many of these chemicals. DDT, for instance, has been banned for many years, but traces of it remain in treated soil and water. And the thousands of other registered chemicals will also be with us—in the soil, the water table and our lakes and streams—for a long time. By being an ecological gardener, you are at least fighting against the chemical onslaught. But don't be surprised if somehow, somewhere, no matter how hard you try, these pernicious toxics find a way into your garden.

Do you know if the nursery or plant breeder where you buy plants uses chemicals? If so, which ones? For this reason, I've tried in recent years to grow some of the more interesting plants from seed, or by trading with other organic gardeners.

But if you can't always do this, encourage your nursery to use as many alternatives to toxic chemicals as possible.

Rule of thumb in the garden: If you learn about some new bug or disease, you'll suddenly find it lurking about your garden. It's true. No disease touched my garden until I started studying them. Then, all of a sudden, there they were right under my nose. My general theory had been that if a plant was fussy, it probably didn't want to live with me. But as I've raised more and more plants, I've become quite possessive about them. I don't want slugs and earwigs munching away on them, and I certainly don't want them contracting unnecessary diseases. The very best way to keep disease out of the garden is to follow a few sensible rules:

• Healthy soil is imperative. It will help keep disease away.
• The next most important factor is compost—rotted compost at that. The components in compost are anathema to fungal diseases and some bacterial diseases. Low-temperature compost, though it takes much longer to produce, has even more disease-resistant elements than does high-temperature compost. You might want to have both kinds if you have the room.
• Mulching keeps the garden clean, protected and constantly fed. In addition, it will help suppress weeds, keep the soil warm at night, cool during the day, and hold in moisture. It also helps prevent damage during freeze-thaw cycles in the winter.

PREVENTATIVE GARDENING

Naturally, prevention is best. If you have healthy soil, it will fight off disease. That means giving it enough water, enough drainage and enough fertilizer. An inch (2.5 centimetres) of compost a year is asking a lot, but that will keep your soil extremely happy.

There are many reasons why your plants might contract an illness. It could be the weather or pollution. The disease might be from a virus, a bacterium or fungus. It's not easy to tell. Diseases come in three forms:

BACTERIAL DISEASES: These are often caused by persistent humidity, wet soil and high temperatures. Bacteria are single-celled micro-organisms that live in both animals and plants. Bacteria that live on dead plants are called saprophytes. Those that cause diseases are parasites or pathogens. They move through the soil in water or when the soil is disturbed. They can enter plants through wounds or natural openings and swim with the sap. Be sure to wash your tools with a bleach solution (one part bleach to four parts water). If you touch diseased plants, wash your hands so you don't spread the disease. Get rid of diseased leaves. Mulching can reduce the spread of bacterial disease. Bacterial diseases can cause:

Rot: Slimy leaves, branches, tubers.

Wilt: Pathogens block the vascular system.

Gall: Overgrowth of cells affected by pathogens.

FUNGAL DISEASES: Fungi take their energy from organic matter. They feed on live matter parasitically and are real trouble-makers. Those that live on dead matter are saprophytic and are helpful in breaking down material. Naturally occurring fungi keep many insect populations under control. Fungal diseases include:

Downy mildew: Powdery patches on leaves.

Powdery mildew: Fungi live on the surface and suck out nutrients from there.

Rust fungi: Pustules of colour.

Leaf spot fungi: Yellow to green spots.

Fungal diseases spread slowly over weeks. In fact, by the time you notice some of them, it's almost too late. Sanitation is your first line of defence against fungal diseases, because the spores can winter over in dead leaves and reinfect the plant.

GREEN TIPS
TREATING FUNGAL DISEASES

- As a preventative, use fungicides on plants that had a fungal disease the year before. You might tag them or make a list to help you remember. Sulphur rock will prevent germination of some fungal spores, but the sulphur must be on the plants before the spores land. Rain washes sulphur rock off plants.
- If temperatures are below 80°F (27°C), you can use sulphur rock every two weeks. It only works where it hits, so be sure to cover the whole plant, the undersides of leaves included.
- Use manure tea and spray the whole plant.
- Water vulnerable plants deeply during the spring. If the roots get too dry and there is a heavy dew, fungi have the perfect opportunity to get started.
- Don't cram plants too close together. Thin out surplus stems of plants such as Michaelmas daisies. Air must get around all the stems.
- Spread cornmeal around the infected area: 2 pounds (1 kilogram) for 100 square feet (9.3 square metres).
- Or try using cornmeal juice: 1 cup (250 millilitres) in 1 gallon (4 litres) water; strain and spray.
- Get badly infected sections of plants right out of the garden. Do not compost them.

VIRAL DISEASES: These are the most difficult to diagnose. No one is sure whether they are living organisms or non-living chemicals, according to Rodale's *Encyclopedia of Organic Gardening*, because they can behave either way. Plants can get viruses from people, insects, tools or anything else that comes in contact with soil or plants. Yellowing, leaf curl or bare branches might mean that a plant has a viral disease. A viral disease that affects many plants is mosaic. Mosaic: Growth is stunted and leaves are mottled green and yellow from chlorosis (loss of chlorophyll).

GREEN TIPS
DIY SOLUTIONS TO COMBAT DISEASES

- **Baking soda:** A good preventative. If you have plants susceptible to powdery mildew. Spray weekly with 1 tablespoon (15 millilitres) baking soda and 1/4 tsp (1.5 millilitres) liquid soap mixed in a gallon (4 litres) of water.
- **Elderberry leaves:** To combat mildew, make an infusion by soaking overnight; sprinkle over roses and other flowers to combat blight.
- **Epsom salts:** To combat mildew, make a spray with 4 tablespoons (60 milli- litres) Epsom salts to 4 cups (1 litre) water. Or try borax and water in the same proportions.
- **Liquid or powdered sulphur:** Makes a good fungicide. Spray on leaves; repeat after a rain. Fungal spores can't germinate in the film it creates.
- **Manure tea:** Also a good fungal fighter (black spot, mildew and rust). Mix well-rotted manure with water (1:5) and use in a spray bottle. The solids that sink to the bottom of the bottle can be used as a fertilizer.
- **Rhubarb:** Boil leaves and sprinkle the tea on soil before sowing and it will prevent clubroot. This is also useful against greenfly and black spot on roses.
- **Seaweed spray:** Strengthens cell walls to fight off fungal spores.

- **Vinegar:** A good fungicide. Dilute 2 tablespoons (30 milli-litres) of cider vinegar in 2 pints (1 litre) of water and spray on leaves.

DEFICIENCIES

If it appears that some disease is affecting your plant, maybe you are giving it too much or too little of something. Your soil is often the best way to cure a sick plant. After you've checked that a plant has the right light requirement, enough water and mulch, consider the following as potential sources of the problem and take corrective action:

LACK OF NITROGEN: Signs: Leaves lose their normal green colour and turn pale. They might turn pale if you've added organic matter before the poor thing was mature enough. The bacteria will use up the nitrogen in the decomposition process, thus starving the plant.

Spindly yellow leaves are another sign of nitrogen deficiency. As the plant gets older, the leaves turn reddish or purple and fall off prematurely. Use a little nitrogen and, if this happens late in the year, make a note to add more next season.

Treatment: To boost nitrogen, give your plants a hit of any of the following: hoof and horn meal, blood meal or well-rotted manure (though this is lower than the other two in nitrogen content).

LACK OF PHOSPHORUS: Signs: Leaves turn reddish, blue-green or purple; are weak; are attacked by insects or disease; or have brown spots.

Treatment: Add bone meal, organic matter, rock phosphates, fish emulsion or well-finished compost.

LACK OF POTASSIUM: Signs: Stunted growth in stems and roots with poor development of flowers, fruits and seeds; leaf colour may be bluish with browning leaf tips; lower leaves turn yellow between veins; brown spots develop; leaves turn brown at the edges or curl up.

Treatment: For yellowing leaves, try dolomitic limestone, or just side dress with compost. Or add wood ashes, granite dust, finely ground potash rocks or sheep manure. Calcium or magnesium will help make potassium available to plants.

LACK OF IRON: Signs: Yellowed leaves in acid-loving plants.

Treatment: Add blood meal, manure or a high-nitrogen material such as peat moss, oak leaves, pine needles or finely powdered sulphur. Rusty nails around the roots of roses will help keep them healthy. Change the colour of the blossoms of wisteria from white to purple by adding rusty nails or iron filings.

LACK OF TRACE MINERALS:

- Compost will provide copper, zinc, manganese and zinc.
- Lack of magnesium: leaves turn yellow, die and fall off. Leaves are necessary to form chlorophyll, so take action to diagnose the problem if leaves fall in significant numbers. Add a handful of Epsom salts around each plant.
- Lack of calcium: distortion and rolling of younger leaves; poor root development. Add gypsum (calcium sulphate).

ADDITIONAL SIGNS:

Yellowing leaves could also mean that there's a lack of light or of certain nutrients, or that temperatures are simply too high for the plant to withstand.

Yellowing between leaf veins could also mean that there's an infestation of spider mites or that pollution is affecting the plant.

Dead areas on leaves or tips could mean that there's too much boron in the soil, too much fluoride in your water supply (in which case let the water sit for at least an hour before using) or an infestation of spider mites.

Spots on leaves could be a sign of leafminer larvae.

Spots on edges and inner sections of leaves could be caused by cool temperatures, cold water, air pollution or too much light.

Now, having said all that, too much of a good thing can also harm your plants. Adding too many amendments (manure) to the top of the soil might make it too rich for plants. With peonies, for instance, dress with manure and bone meal, but make sure the mixture doesn't come in contact with the crown. Irises are prone to crown rot so use rock phosphate and bone meal, but no manure. Blood meal makes a rich soil. Keep that in mind when you're sprinkling it around bulbs to keep squirrels away.

SPECIFIC DISEASES

BLACK SPOT ON ROSES:

Symptoms: Reddish to black spots appear on the leaves, which turn yellow and fall off. At the beginning, a few spots appear, then little, black, pimply-type lesions; this means the spores are about to take off. Get them first because they weaken plants (which need the leaves to produce food for the blooms).

GREEN TIPS
DEFEATING BLACK SPOT

- Plant parsley near roses to keep off black spot.
- Spray roses with 2 tablespoons (30 millilitres) baking soda mixed in 1 gallon (4 litres) of water with a drop of detergent.

- Don't plant too many roses prone to this disease together. Mix up varieties that are tolerant with those that are intolerant. Be sure to have healthy plants in the first place.
- Get all the leaves off the soil as quickly as they fall. They must not stay in the garden; bag and remove.
- In spring, prune out any canes that look sickly.
- Don't water from overhead, and mulch generously to keep rain or hose water from splashing on leaves. Water early in the day.

BOTRYTIS:

Symptoms: This is a fungus that produces fuzzy grey mould. At first, it looks like water marks on the leaves, stems or even the flowers. In a few days, mould appears and that means anything affected is starting to rot. The saprophytic fungi can overwinter. And, alas, almost any plant can get this.

GREEN TIPS
TREATING BOTRYTIS:

- Botrytis is a blight that often hits peonies. The new leaf shoots wilt when they are about 1 foot (30 centimetres) high. The spores can infect buds, flowers and leaves. The buds turn black. Cut all foliage to the ground and get it out of the garden—not into the compost.
- As a last-ditch effort, spray it with Bordeaux mixture (copper sulphate and lime) when the shoots hit about 10 inches (25 centimetres). Repeat at least twice. Lift any infected crowns in the fall, dig out the rotted parts and dip the rest in the same Bordeaux mixture. Replant and give a good hit of compost.
- Make sure the plants have sufficient air circulation.

- Pick off infected leaves and get rid of them.
- If the problem continues, a good idea is to remove the top 2 inches (5 centimetres) of soil around the plant and replace it completely.
- Avoid overhead watering.

MILDEW:

Symptoms: Mildew manifests itself in white powdery stuff on the leaves and shoots. It stunts growth.

This could mean that the roots have dried out. I find this happens regularly with pulmonarias—I usually have them near ferns and hostas, which grab the moisture. The leaves curl up when the roots are dry.

GREEN TIPS
DEALING WITH MILDEW

- Remove the affected leaves; give the plant a good soaking; then mulch with compost.
- Garlic is a natural fungicide; plant it next to plants prone to this disease.
- Use a baking soda spray: 1 tablespoon (15 millilitres) baking soda with 1/2 teaspoon (2.5 millilitres) soap in 1 gallon (4 litres) of water.
- Phlox seems particularly susceptible in the eastern part of the country—watch the lower leaves. Make sure the plants are in a sunny place with good air circulation.
- Spray milk on plants suffering from mildew or mould.

RUST:

Symptoms: Raised coloured pustules disfigure leaves, which dry up and fall. Sienna-coloured spores can overwinter, so clean up everything affected very carefully.

GREEN TIPS
PREVENTING AND TREATING RUST

- Provide lots of space for each plant and keep the soil moist.
- Use a commercial sulphur spray and follow the directions carefully.
- Get rid of seriously infected plants.

WILT:

Symptoms: Obvious wilting appears first in leaves as the fungi travel through the vascular system of the plant and plug it.

GREEN TIPS
WHAT TO DO ABOUT WILT:

- Wilt, a fungal disease, often affects clematis. Injury from a lawn mower or from cultivating can cause the plant to die back, but if there are no obvious injuries, the problem could be wilt. The disease produces reddish lesions around the stems, which then proceed to wither away. Prune radically as soon as you notice the top growth going this way. Cut back to 6 inches (15 centimetres) above ground. Get rid of prunings safely.

NEMATODES:

Test on your own this way: Take soil samples from different places in the garden at a depth of about 6 inches (15 centimetres). Mix them up and divide into six pots. Put three in the freezer for three or four days. Plant several fast-growing seeds such as radishes. Cover with coir and keep in a warm place to germinate. If the freezer soil is significantly better than the non-freezer soil, you probably have nematodes in the garden.

6

WEEDS

FRIENDS OR FOES?

No matter how long I garden, weeds continue to stump me. I'm always so grateful to see stuff come up in spring that I'm willing to let anything grow. Then comes the shock of having to weed. I usually let a plant grow until it's got a few leaves because I think I'll be able to identify friend or foe. Ha! I usually forget; then it means getting out weed identification books, but that never seems to help. Instead, I go to the messiest, most unkempt garden in the neighbourhood. If something's growing there, I probably don't want it in my garden. I may lose a few flowers but not many.

Of course, there are plants considered weeds I adore—the wild aster, for instance, has a place in my garden as does Queen-Anne's lace (which has the benefit of attracting parasitic wasps that rid the garden of aphids) and a clump of goldenrod for fall colour.

What's a weed? You could say it's any plant that's come unbidden, and is invasive. By taking this view, you won't be upset by a few weeds lurking about. I once tried transplanting Queen-Anne's lace. No luck. But one year it appeared on its own. The seed might have been dropped by a bird or moved in by an insect.

Weeds don't grow everywhere but they do seem to thrive in places that are cultivated. This makes them less than wild in many cases. They are extremely well-adapted plants; opportunistic is probably a better word. They will move into any niche left open to them. Weeds form an intricate community of plants. They can change the environment of your plants; and the kinds of weeds will change as the environment changes. For instance, some weeds will increase seed production like wildfire if there is enough space between similar plants. Other weeds have, over millennia, come to imitate the crops they invade. There is a weed corn; a grass that looks like rice until it flowers; and lamb's-quarters will grow prostrate rather than upright to imitate neighbouring plants. Janine Benyus has written an important book, *Biomimicry*, about these complex plant relationships.

Most weeds are non-native plants—not all native plants are weeds by a long shot. Natives have been here since Day One of plant history. Most weeds or the plants we consider weeds and therefore A Bad Thing are introductions—even if hundreds of years old. They were brought over by the first waves of Europeans in ships, on shoes, in pockets. Some by accident, some by design.

Weeds can be prodigious producers of seeds. Some put out hundreds of thousands per plant. And that's one of the reasons we're unhappy about them. They tend to take over everything else in their lust for survival. And many can wait for years, decades, even a hundred years, to germinate. So you never know when the little devils will spring up again. With the acceleration of climate change, scientists are predicting that weeds will become more virulent and will produce a lot more pollen than they have in the past, so we will have to become more vigilant in our removal of the pesky ones.

What weeds might do is sap nutrients from the very plants you want to keep healthy. Some exude toxins from their roots, stems or leaves, thus affecting the growth of flowers and shrubs nearby. This is called allelopathy. Other weeds may overwinter diseases and pests.

Weeds aren't necessarily invasive, terrible things. They've been given a bum rap—many of them are very useful. Low, mat-forming weeds can keep the ground cool around vegetables, trees and shrubs. They can also hold nutrients in bare soil. Others attract beneficial insects or even act as trap crops, easy to handpick them. Really deep-rooted perennial weeds will break up hardpan that's as tough as concrete, drawing nutrients that are deep in the soil to a much higher level. They can bring moisture to the surface under the most adverse conditions. The root systems of many weeds also provide channels for more domesticated plants. In other words, they can create the right conditions in which other plants will flourish. When they die, they provide the soil with organic matter.

You can have weeds growing side-by-side with crops or flowers quite successfully. In many cases, they make great companions. But there are a few caveats in this. You've got a problem if you have weeds such as bindweed and quackgrass—they will smother or choke everything around them. Bindweed roots are very deep and can put out runners 3 to 9 feet (1 to 3 metres) long. If you attack them at the root, you help them proliferate. Keep cutting the tops off until the root is starved and dies. Shallow-rooted weeds such as chickweed, on the other hand, will shade seedlings. Having a few weeds in bare spots will hold in moisture, protect your plants and, most important, give bugs something to munch on.

One of the many reasons that weeds may move in on your territory is that your soil is not as fertile as it once was. Add lots of organic matter to improve the soil and help the soil get rid of the pest weeds.

GREEN TIPS
HOW TO DEAL WITH WEEDS:

- Clear your space of weeds before planting and put down a mulch from 2 to 4 inches (5 to 10 centimetres) thick.
- Place plants close together without crowding root systems—the less space you leave bare, the less likely it is that weeds will invade. Be careful about doing this with plants that hate being moved when they reach maturity.
- Pull weeds until new plants are established, then weed every three or four weeks after that.
- Don't let annual weeds develop seedheads. Chickweed and lamb's-quarters, for example, put out thousands of seeds from one plant. Cultivate the soil and mulch.
- If you're sure you've got a tonne of weeds in one section of your garden, solarize it: Dig up the area, rake and then cover the surface with dark plastic. This will starve weed seeds of the light they need to germinate.
- If you are planting seeds or seedlings, make sure you mark them so you know which are friends. After each rain, get out there and pick away at the green stuff between markers.
- Pulling out perennial weeds such as bindweed or twitch grass, will just encourage them; by tilling, you'll help spread them. Use heavy layers of mulch if they are a real pain. Keep topping them off until the roots are starved.

- Keep mowing on a regular basis and cutting off tops until there's a killing frost.
- If you're making a new bed and you can't install plants immediately, put in a cover crop such as clover or alfalfa to help keep weeds down and protect the soil.
- Pour boiling water over weeds in cracks—it will help kill them and keep seeds from germinating. This really works well. I've managed to keep our brick walk clear without using herbicides.
- If you've got weed seeds in your mulch or compost, try the following method to eliminate them: during the fall, spread the material out on the ground, water and cover with black plastic. The weeds will germinate and be killed off by frost and darkness.
- Cover the weed-infested area with newspapers topped off with heavy mulch and just let it sit for a year.
- With many weeds such as thistles, wait until after a heavy rain and pull them out by the roots.
- If you are ridding your garden of poison ivy or poison oak, don't burn the remains (poison fumes) and be sure to wear protective clothing. Pull them out the minute you see that telltale three-leaf formation. Remove whole plants in fall when they turn brilliant red. If any of this stuff gets on your body, wash it off with alcohol, water and a bit of chlorine bleach. Wash this off with an alkaline-based soap.

BENEFICIAL WEEDS

Weeds attract spiders, which prey on insect pests. Spiders are a natural insect filter in the garden and will allow plants to flourish. They reduce leafhoppers, aphids, leafworm and spider mites. If you have space, leave a 3-foot (1-metre) strip of wild, undisturbed vegetation. Some weeds stimulate the growth of valuable organisms in the soil.

The following are good weeds (A = annual; B = biennial; P = perennial):

Buttercup (P): This plant retards growth of nitrogen bacteria; will kill off clover; also discourages most other plants if you have something you want to get rid of.

Chickweed (P): This herb is rich in copper; eat it the same way you do cress.

Clover (P): Plant clover, which has beautiful scented flowers, instead of grass and you will add nitrogen to the soil; this cover crop is far easier to tend than grass.

Couch grass (P): This is a good source of potassium for the compost; you can also mulch with it; don't let it go to seed.

Dandelion (P): Although despised by many people, this weed has beautiful deep roots that bring nutrients up from deep in the soil. If you want hardpan broken up, these plants will do the job. Tolerate a few and learn to appreciate the young leaves in salads. They cleanse the blood and improve the enamel on your teeth. Other flowers welcome them since they aid growth. They are good for adding iron and copper to the compost, and they make an excellent liquid fertilizer for foliar feeding. Gather early in the morning and cover with water; bring to a boil; cool and strain. Dilute 1:4 with water, add a bit of liquid soap and blend.

Fleabane (P): The oil from this plant repels mosquitoes and, presumably, fleas.

Lamb's-quarters (P): This is a good trap plant for aphids, which attract ladybugs. A purply-red patina indicates a nitrogen deficiency in the soil. You can eat the leaves—a good source of vitamin A. This plant is also high in iron, protein, vitamins B1 and B2, and calcium. Allow it to grow near your tomato patch along with pigweed and sow thistle and you'll get a much better crop. They will also help plants withstand drought. Adds strength to the following flowers: marigolds, peonies and pansies.

Lamb's quarters (*Chenopodium album*): The fresh young greens of this common garden weed can be eaten as salad.

Milkweed (P): This is an important nectar source for bees and butterflies; larval food for the monarch butterfly. Grows in dry soil. The juice from the plant cures warts—so they say. It traps cutworms for easy picking. Although it's really hard to get established, once established it looks after itself.

Mullein (P): This is another dramatic plant that can, if controlled, look good in the garden. You can get rid of it by cutting out the root below the crown. It indicates you have dry soil. Moth mullein is particularly pretty.

Nettle (P): Both false and stinging nettles, when young, can be eaten in salads. They fend off slugs and snails. Nettle is excellent for the compost pile—it is a great activator and will speed things up if your heap seems a bit sluggish. To control, pull out the roots or mow regularly. Use gloves when you're handling this plant.

Ox-eye daisy (P): I like this pretty plant. If you have too many, pull out by the roots. This will keep them under control and you'll be able to enjoy the cut flowers.

Purslane (P): The yellow flowers are really quite pretty (purslane is a member of the portulaca family). The flowers only open when the sun is out. Use young leaves and flowers in salads. If you have too many plants, pull them out. Don't put them in the composter.

Queen-Anne's lace (B): This attractive plant is both hardy and spreads quickly, so you may end up with a serious infestation. But I like it anyway and keep it confined to one plant, deadheading scrupulously. It attracts parasitic wasps, which eat aphids.

Queen-Anne's lace (*Daucus carota*): A European biennial now at home in fields and along roadsides throughout the country is also known as wild carrot.

Shepherd's purse (P): You'll recognize this one by its seed capsule, which gives off a viscous compound. Aquatic insects stick to it; it can be used for mosquito larvae control.

WEEDS FOR EATING: Dandelion, milkweed, purslane, sheep sorrel, wild lettuce.

NASTY WEEDS

Annual weeds can generally be controlled by using a smothering mulch from 2 to 4 inches (5 to 10 centimetres) thick.

Bindweed (P): Although beautiful, this twining plant is a real killer. Keep cutting it off—pulling it up by the roots will just make it proliferate. It will take a few years to get rid of it. Hack away at anything that insinuates itself above ground. Solarize infected areas.

Chickweed (A): Edible when young, this weed self-seeds and creeps along. Keep pulling up and put in composter.

Cocklebur (A): This is poisonous to some animals, so keep it mowed.

Crabgrass (A): This grows by stolons or creeping stems. It isn't crazy about good soil, so improve your soil.

Deadly nightshade (A): The berries are poisonous and the plant attracts pests and diseases; keep pulling it out.

Horse nettle (P): To control this weed, don't allow seeds to form. Cover with sod.

Jimson weed (A): Rich, well-drained soil is the medium of choice for this plant, which is poisonous. Cut it back before it seeds, then get rid of all parts of the plant.

Knotweed (A): An infestation may mean the soil is too compacted, so keep soil hoed and add manure. Chop back and solarize.

Purple loosestrife (P): Another European introduction, this is a beauty of a plant. Alas, it has escaped into wetlands, cutting out the food supply that marsh birds depend on. And it's taking over the countryside, diminishing biodiversity. Once it's done a bunko into the wild, it really fits the category of weed. You must be very careful to control it. Even the cultivars aren't completely trustworthy. If you do plant the cultivars 'Morden's Gleam,' 'Morden Pink' or 'Morden Rose,' you must keep them deadheaded and away from wet areas. Recent research shows that the hybrids produce seeds that are even more virulent when they reach the wild. I've been avoiding this plant with regret.

Purple loosestrife (*Lythrum salicaria*): Let loose in wetlands, this garden perennial chokes out native vegetation.

Plantain (P): This is usually a sign of compacted soil, so aerate the soil. Add lots of compost or manure. It was once known as White Man's Footprint.

Quack-grass (P): Although it binds loose soil and prevents erosion on slopes, it can choke out most other plants. It likes acid soil and increases by seed and underground stems (rhizomes). It grows fast; roots can travel 60 feet (16.2 metres) laterally. Keep removing top growth, hacking away at it with a sharp hoe. Spade up in fall and expose the rhizomes, then pull by hand. Leave a heavy mulch on top for a season.

Ragweed (A): Don't get this plant mixed up with goldenrod. Ragweed is the one that affects those with hay fever. Its pollen is so light that it will travel as high as a seven-storey building. Keep it mowed close to the ground for control.

Smartweed (A): This is a real spreader. Keep it mowed.

Thistles (P): Russian thistle should be pulled out or mowed down. Canada thistle must be dug out by the root—completely out—or it will start new plants. They're good for the compost because they add potassium. Don't let thistles flower.

Twitch grass (P): Tilling spreads it, so be very careful.

WEED INDICATORS

Plants act as indicators of what's going on in the soil. Weeds are no different. They may indicate that your soil is exhausted, is becoming increasingly acidic or lacks sufficient humus. When whole families of weeds move in, it means there is a profound decline in the health or balance of the soil.

If you have any of the plants listed here, they may indicate the following kinds of soil:

Acid soil: Cinquefoil, sheep sorrel, spurrey, swamp horsetail, dock, knapweed, bracken, buttercup, hawkweed, nettles.

Slightly acid soil: Black-eyed Susan, chickweed, daisy,

yarrow. They could also mean that there is lack of air or poor drainage.

Alkaline soil: Goldenrod, saltbush, saltwort, bladder campion, white mustard, sow thistle.

Sandy soil: Goldenrod, broom sedge, wild lettuce, onion, yellow toadflax, partridge pea.

Limestone soil: Chamomile, pennycress, peppergrass, wormseed.

Rich soil: Burdock, ground ivy, lamb's-quarters, pigweed, purslane, chickweed, buttercup, dandelions, nettles. All these weeds love to be in cultivated soil.

Poorly drained soil: Bindweed, cutgrass, docks, foxtail grass, Joe-Pye weed, hedge nettle, horsetail, meadow pink, ox-eye daisy, St. John's wort, silverweed, smartweed, spiderwort.

Hardpan soil: Bindweed, chamomile, horse nettle, morning glory, field mustard, pennycress, quack-grass, plantain. These weeds indicate that there is too much potash in the soil.

My last comment here is about goutweed, which will spread up to 80 feet (24 metres)—and every time you try to dig it out, a new mother plant will spring up. The ONLY thing that will get rid of it is constant cutting back to the ground and solarizing it. Confine this plant to a container in deep shade or on a hopeless bare slope.

Ecological gardening means having a balance between what you pull out and what you leave in. Having weeds in the garden doesn't mean that you are a lazy or sloppy gardener. Recognize the ones that are beneficial and keep them. Pull, mulch, chop the rest. But don't kill them with chemicals.

7

PLANTING

❀

COMPANIONS FOR LIFE

For a terrible period in my life, I didn't have control over my garden. I rented out the first floor of our duplex to people who swore they loved to garden. I watched as year after year my plants were swamped by what I referred to as those funny-looking tomato plants: hemp, also known as marijuana. What I didn't know at this time of great despair was that this plant excretes certain pathogenic micro-organisms that were not destroying but protecting the other plants and improving the health of the soil. I'm not in any way recommending that you plant these—they are illegal. It's by way of illustrating that plants perform the most astonishing functions. They have properties that we are just now beginning to recognize.

Native people thousands of years ago recognized this fact and also that planting in communities was mutually beneficial for plants. The Three Sisters—corn, beans and squash—illustrate this perfectly. People planted corn seed in hills, but not too close together. Tall corn gave the bean plant something to climb up; the squash ran along the ground and kept weeds out and moisture in, and fixed nitrogen in the soil. The fields were surrounded with sunflowers so that the birds would have something to eat and stay away from the corn. It all worked perfectly within its own self-organizing ecosystem.

One of the major aspects of ecological gardening is planting properly—right plant, right place. A carved-in-stone rule is that you always put a plant in the area where its major needs will be met: a bog-loving plant in a damp area; a shade-loving plant in the right density of shade (light, deep, dappled or semi-shade). This may seem insultingly obvious, but you'd be surprised what people try to do to plants.

Try some or all of the suggestions set out below. The eco logical gardener is going to be looking at wild roadsides, woods and meadows for inspiration. If you are ever in doubt about what you're doing in the garden, you can't go wrong by echoing what you see growing naturally around you. When we get rid of the idea that we're here to dominate our environment and, instead, take on the responsibility of working with it, we'll bring Nature closer to ourselves.

There are many pluses to working in this way. Your garden will have much greater diversity in the kind and number of plants. Disease and insect problems will diminish when you achieve this in your garden.

COMPANION PLANTING

I never really believed in companion planting until the year Queen-Anne's lace appeared in my garden. One day I saw ladybugs on it and realized they loved this plant. From then on my garden has had at least one Queen-Anne's lace and a huge population of ladybugs. I learned more about this useful, beautiful bug: they like daisies, butterfly weed, tansy, cosmos and fennel. In order to please, I planted them all.

The ancients, of course, found magical properties in herbs and many other plants. And we are just beginning to tap this rich source of information. After composting, the second biggest favour you can do your garden is to put the right plants together. You can inoculate your soil, boost its health and aerate it by putting in certain plants. The perfect mix will include companions planted to protect one another.

Companion planting can provide shade, protection from the wind, proper humidity and support, or keep bugs and disease away. Instead of letting the plants compete with each other and have only the strongest survive, you can control this competition.

GREEN TIPS
GUIDELINES FOR COMPANION PLANTING:

- Put sun-lovers in front of those demanding less light. One can live very happily in the shade of the other.
- Put very deep-rooted plants next to ones with shallow roots.
- Plants with big roots can break up the soil for those with more shallow roots and bring up minerals from deep in the soil.
- Put plants that bloom early next to those that bloom later for a continuous display or crop.
- Put in heavy feeders first—they like lots of water and food—then follow later on with those requiring light feeding. Give them both lashings of compost. Peonies and delphiniums, for instance, are great gobblers, but most herbs are light feeders.
- Don't crowd plants. If you're trying for an instant show, use annuals. Don't shove perennials up against each

other. You'll only inhibit growth and future health.

- Give trees and shrubs lots of room, but plant shade-loving, shallow-rooted plants beneath them.
- Plant by allelopathy. Some plants exude chemicals from their roots to either inhibit or encourage the growth of other plants.
- Don't plant things together that attract the same insects and diseases.
- Aromatic plants that repel pests can protect those with little scent.
- Plant early bloomers with plants that do not bear flowers until late in the season (or that are not allowed to flower). This will provide pollen and nectar for some insect predators and parasitoids (insects that parasitize other insects).
- Combine plants that stimulate biological activity in the soil with crops that are heavy feeders.

PLANTS TO ATTRACT BEES: You want bees in your garden because they will pollinate your flowers. Bees aren't necessarily attracted to scented flowers; they love blue plants, which often don't have any perfume. Good bee-attracting perennials include: wallflower, arabis, borage, all the campanulas, catmint, heather and heaths, thymes, honeysuckle, lavender, lemon balm, daphne, sunflower, butterfly weed, scabious, asters, roses (particularly rugosa roses) and caryopteris. Annuals include cleome, calendula, nasturtium and white alyssum.

PLANTS TO ATTRACT BUTTERFLIES: Plants with nectar will attract butterflies. They love yellow and purple blossoms; they don't like white roses. Flowers to attract butterflies include Joe-Pye weed, candytuft, mignonette, zinnias, phlox, portulaca,

PLANTING: Companions for Life

alyssum, wallflowers, sweet rocket and sweet William. Grow a butterfly bush—*a butterfly magnet*. It's also important to plant host plants for butterfly larvae: herbs (dill and parsley), weeds (goldenrod, clover, milkweed, dandelions) and willow or birch trees, for example.

PROTECTIVE BOTANICALS

Now here's a real horticultural buzzword—botanicals. Protective botanicals are plants that secrete an odour or an oil from their roots which attracts or repels bugs or diseases. Don't expect an instant reaction, however. Marigolds, for instance, discourage nematodes, but you might have to plant a lot of them a couple of years in a row to get results.

TRAP PLANTS: Many plants act as traps—that is, they attract an insect away from other plants so that it's easy to pick the creatures off the trap plant.
- If you plant nasturtiums near tomato plants, aphids will be enticed away from the tomatoes to the nasturtiums.
- Mustard also attracts insects, so when they lay their eggs, it's easy to destroy plant and eggs.
- Columbines attract spider mites.
- Milkweed can be used as a trap crop for cutworms.

REPELLENTS: Some plants are repellents rather than traps.
- Citronella is the most obvious—it keeps mosquitoes at bay—but there's also pennyroyal, thyme, lavender, winter-green, anise, bay, ginkgo, elder and pyrethrum.
- Mexican bean beetle is repelled by marigold, potato, rosemary, summer savoury and petunia.
- Insecticidal flowers include asters, chrysanthemums, cosmos, coreopsis, nasturtiums and French and Mexican

marigolds. Plant them throughout the garden to discourage pests.

- Spider mites are repelled by onions and garlic chives.

SOME PLANTS AND THEIR SPECIAL PROPERTIES:

- Anise and coriander germinate better if planted together.
- Bee balm planted with tomatoes really does improve their flavour, but watch out—bee balm can spread quickly.
- Birch excretes substances that encourage fermentation of compost and manure; place your bin about 6 feet (2 metres) away from the tree.
- Borage contains potassium, calcium and other minerals and is an excellent companion for strawberries.
- Catnip leaves steeped in water and used as a tea will keep flea beetle away.
- Chamomile can be used against fleas; soak blossoms for two days. It also makes a good spray to combat diseases.
- Chives act as a fungicide. Plant near roses to help keep them healthy.
- Elder is a wonderful tree. It not only attracts birds, but also has other uses. Bruise the leaves and drag elder branches across a seedbed to discourage maggots.
- If you have horsetail in your garden, don't despair. Make a spray: dry horsetail; then cover with cold water; boil for 10 minutes. Cool and strain. Dilute with water, 1:20.
- Dandelions are natural humus producers and earthworms like them. Their 3-foot (1-metre) roots bring minerals, especially calcium, from beneath hardpan and deposit them closer to the surface. Earthworms use the root channels to go deeper into the soil; they exhale ethylene gas, which encourages early maturity in nearby plants.

- Delphiniums contain alkaloids which can cause dermatitis; so do euphorbias.
- False indigo is repellent to chinch bugs and striped cucumber beetles; its powdered pods and seeds are toxic to Mexican bean beetle larvae. A sugar derivative from this plant is effective against chinch bugs, cotton aphids, squash bugs, tarnished plant bugs, potato leafhoppers, blister beetles, and spotted cucumber beetles.
- Fennel hates wormwood, so don't plant them close together.
- Feverfew planted around your garden will discourage bugs. Tuck it under other plants. It thrives in light or shade, so you have to be careful it doesn't take over.
- Plant flowering cabbage and kale with mint, thyme, rosemary, sage and hyssop.
- Four-o'clock has poisonous foliage but Japanese beetles love to eat it. The fact that they then kick the bucket doesn't seem to discourage them.
- Garlic is a splendid food plant—fresh garlic is incomparable—and it has many other uses as well. For instance, it keeps mice away from roses and lilies; planted near strawberries, it deters nematodes and mould.
- Mince garlic in a food processor; mix with water and a little vegetable oil. This spray discourages insects and blights and acts like an antibiotic on plants. Never plant garlic near gladioli—they don't like each other at all.
- Geraniums (pelargoniums—the colourful annuals you are used to seeing) are useful planted with roses since they'll discourage Japanese beetles.
- Hyssop planted with grape vines will increase the crop.
- Hyssop, lemon balm and valerian are helpful to many vegetables.
- Lamb's-quarters planted near zinnias, marigolds, peonies or

pansies will make them much more vigorous. It improves the soil. This plant plays host to ladybirds but is subject to leafminer (whose larvae the ladybirds love).

- Larkspur is effective against aphids and thrips. Its pow- dered roots are toxic to bean leafroller, cross-striped cab- bageworms, cabbage loopers and melon worms.
- Lovage inhibits the growth of nearby plants.
- Lupines add calcium to the soil; plant near peonies, monkshood, elecampane, Michaelmas daisies, iris, daylilies and stocks.
- Marigolds repel nematodes and are useful with chrysan themums, calendula and dahlias. They discourage pests around fruit trees. Plant under tomatoes as a soil covering.
- Nasturtiums planted around apple trees repel woolly aphids and cucumber beetles. Plant near broccoli to repel aphids.
- Nettle helps plants withstand lice, slugs and snails. It also helps with growth of mint and tomatoes and will increase the scent of herbs.
- Parsley planted near bulbs, tomatoes and roses will protect them against black spot.
- Pennyroyal is reputed to repel pests in the garden and fleas from a cat. Some gardeners absolutely swear by it, but I've found that this plant is often mis-identified in nurseries, so be very careful when you buy it. Try it in a container first and if it's the pretty ground cover, put it in the garden.
- Pepper juice inoculates plants against viruses borne by wind or bugs. Plant hot peppers to discourage insects.
- Petunias repel leafhoppers; so do geraniums.
- Pyrethrum is the natural source of many insecticides. Make your own by putting the flowers through a food processor and adding water. Strain and use as a spray.
- Rue planted with roses will discourage Japanese beetle.

Cats hate the scent so if they are tearing up the furniture, rub some rue on a cloth and drape over the favoured area. Don't plant with basil.
- Salad burnet is rich in magnesium.
- Scotch broom accumulates calcium in the soil.
- Sheep sorrel takes up phosphorus.
- Tansy planted next to berry bushes will keep them happy.
- Wormwood in a spray (boil up the leaves and strain) will discourage slugs on the ground; spray it around vulnerable vegetation in the fall. It makes worms flee and will inhibit the growth of plants nearby. It also protects against rust, so plant near berries.
- Yarrow grown next to herbs enhances their oils.

INDICATOR PLANTS:

Plants give us lots of information if we know what to look for.
- Bachelor's-button has blue blossoms when planted in limestone soil; rose and pink in acid soil. The redder they become, the more acidic your soil.
- Boltonia signals poor drainage.
- Seaside aster indicates the presence of salt in your soil.
- Sorrel indicates a lack of lime in the soil.
- Dandelion, wild mustard and pigweed only grow in fertile, balanced soil.
- Nettles love rich, damp soil.
- Knotweed indicates acid soil.

PLANTING STRATEGIES

Here are more great tricks to help you mix your plants to their best advantage. Think of your garden in storeys: ground covers, low perennials, higher ones, small shrubs, big perennials and shrubs, and then trees. Remember, though, that for every foot

(30 centimetres) a tree grows, its shadow will cast another foot (30 centimetres) of shade on the ground. Everything you add to the mix will change the environment—usually for the better.

SQUARE-FOOT PLANTING: One method of planting is the square-foot method. There is an entire book on the subject (see *Square Foot Gardening* by Mel Bartholomew) and if you've got a real space problem, I recommend it. Each square is planted with something different in blocks 4 feet (1.3 metres) square, with an average of eight plants per square. You have little walkways between each block so you never, ever, step on the soil that you're cultivating.

RAISED BEDS: The intensive method of planting uses raised beds. This increases the air supply to the roots and will extend your planting time and plant range by at least a zone. It's also the best way to solve any problems you may have with poor drainage or crummy soil.

- **Raised bed, good soil:** If you already have good soil, then making a raised bed is simple—just pile it higher than the soil around it (give it a bit of a slope on the edges).
- **Raised bed, poor soil:** If you have poor soil and drainage:
  - Dig down and lay a bed of rocks or junk left over from construction.
  - To construct the sides of the bed, use bricks, stones or wood, almost anything that catches your fancy will do. Just make sure that you'll be able to build up the soil from 8 inches to 3 feet (20 to 90 centimetres) high behind it.
  - Add a layer of gravel mixed with well-soaked coir. If you have compost, add it as well. Add well-dampened newspapers for one layer if the bed is deep enough.
  - Top with good soil that's been well raked.

CHART YOUR COMPANIONS

IF YOU PLANT:	ACCOMPANY IT WITH:
Asparagus	Tomatoes, parsley, basil
Basil	Tomatoes (dislikes rue; repels flies and mosquitoes)
Bee balm	Tomatoes (improves flavour)
Borage	Tomatoes (deters tomato worm); squash, strawberries
Catnip	Anywhere in border (discourages flea beetles)
Chives	Plant around fruit trees (keeps insects off)
Garlic	Roses, raspberries; use everywhere in the garden (enhances essential oils of herbs)
Hyssop	Grapes; potatoes (deters potato beetle)
Lemon balm	Throughout garden, though it can be invasive
Marigold	Throughout garden (keeps out nematodes and many insects)
Marjoram	Throughout garden
Mint	Tomatoes (planted in a container)
Nasturtium	Tomatoes, radishes; under fruit trees (enemy of aphids)
Onion	Strawberries, tomato, lettuce (against onslaught of slugs)
Parsley	Tomatoes, asparagus
Petunia	Throughout garden
Pigweed	Throughout garden (brings nutrients to topsoil)
Pot marigold	Tomatoes; throughout garden (repels many pests)
Radish	Tomatoes, nasturtium (repels many pests)
Rosemary	Sage

Rue	Roses, raspberries (deters Japanese beetle)
Sage	Rosemary (keeps out some insects)
Southernwood	Throughout garden
Strawberry	Borage; lettuce
Tansy	Fruit trees (deters many pests)
Tarragon	Throughout garden
Thyme	Throughout garden
Tomato	Chives, onion, parsley, asparagus, marigold,nasturtium
Valerian	Throughout garden
Wormwood	Throughout garden (keeps animals out)
Yarrow	Herbs (enhances essential oils)

PEST:	PLANT TO REPEL:
Ants	Pennyroyal, spearmint, southernwood, tansy
Aphids	Tansy
Borer	Garlic, tansy, onion
Cutworm	Tansy
Eelworm	French and African marigolds
Flea beetle	Wormwood, mint, catnip
Fruit tree moth	Southernwood
Gopher	Castor bean
Japanese beetle	Garlic, larkspur, tansy, rue, white geraniums
Leafhopper	Petunia, geranium
Mexican bean beetle	Marigold, rosemary, summer savoury, petunia
Mice	Spurge
Mole	Castor bean, mole plant (spurge), squill
Nematode	African and French marigolds, salvia, scarlet, sage, dahlia, calendula, asparagus

Plum curculio	Garlic
Rabbit	Allium
Rose chafer	Geranium, petunia, onion
Slug	Prostrate rosemary, wormwood
Squash bug	Tansy, nasturtium
Striped pumpkin beetle	Nasturtium
Tomato hornworm	Borage, marigold, opal basil
Whitefly	Nasturtium, marigold
Wireworm	White mustard, buckwheat, woad

Source: *Rodale's Encyclopedia of Organic Gardening*

8

WATER AND THE GARDEN

An ecological garden is easy on water. We don't have unlimited supplies of this precious resource and soon most homes will be on water metres and there will be water rationing and fines for leaving sprinklers running for hours. These aren't just threats, they have become a reality in many cities. And not a minute too soon. This is one of the most precious commodities on earth and, at the moment, we have enough but many people have none. Use it as though it was running out.

Even in North America, there are areas going through a desertification process swifter than in some parts of Africa. On the west coast around Los Angeles, the water table has been drastically lowered by gross demand—this is terrifying. Arizona makes you want to weep.

There are a number of things you can do to conserve water. As a start, cut back on the amount of lawn you have. Use drought-tolerant plants, efficient watering systems and mulch.

We can't expect lush landscapes to be an inalienable right. This massive drain on the water supply demands much from the collective imagination. There are a myriad things you can do with even a small patch of land besides grow grass and some petunias. The possibilities are almost infinite in every region of the country—but first acquaint yourself with what you have in front of you.

Try to imagine what the garden was like before all this cultivating, so-called civilizing, started. Think of how beautiful it must have been. We can no longer go back to that state, but we can try to understand the essence of those natural landscapes.

What vegetation is native to your area? What special light do you have? How far can you see—for miles or only up close?

WATERING AND YOUR SOIL

Know your soil—there's no point in following watering instructions for somebody else's soil. The root systems of plants fill out the air holes between the grains of soil. This is where the water goes, providing moisture and oxygen to the roots and the soil below. When a plant doesn't have the right amount of water, it becomes stressed or goes into shock, and sometimes it's terminal.

So figure out what you've got in your garden and follow these general rules:

1. Water long enough for the water to go below the general root level. If you give plants frequent shallow waterings, you will encourage shallow root growth, which leaves them less likely to tolerate drought. It's better to water less often, more deeply.

2. Water plants individually if you can. This way you become sensitive to the needs of each of them.

3. Water early in the morning or late in the afternoon (more on this to come).

To help you determine how often and how much, consider the following:

Sandy soil: If you have sandy soil, water runs through it very quickly. You can add humus to retain some moisture but it's still going to drain too fast. You'll have to water more often, but you won't have to water for a long time. One inch (2.5 centimetres) of rain will penetrate 2 feet (60 centimetres). Sandy soil needs about 2 inches (5 centimetres) a week.

Loam: This is the perfect garden soil—enough humus to hold moisture in the soil, but still has good drainage. You should be so lucky. One inch (2.5 centimetres) of rain will penetrate 16 inches (40 centimetres). Needs about 1/2 to 3/4 inch (1 to 2 centimetres) a week.

Clay soil: The spaces between the soil particles are very close, so water tends to move through it very slowly. You'll have to water for a long time, but not as often since it tends to hold water longer. Water slowly or it will run off in every direction. One inch (2.5 centimetres) of rain will penetrate 11 inches (27.5 centimetres). Clay soil needs about 1 inch (2.5 centimetres) a week.

All of the above, of course, depend on how hot it is, and the season. Keep an eye on your plants. Don't worry if they wilt and then recover at the end of the day. If they stay wilted over a 24-hour period, get out the hose. In spring, water transplants and seedlings by hand. In summer, do general watering. In fall, slow down once the days start to get shorter but be sure to water trees and shrubs well before frost sets in. This is especially true of evergreens, which transpire all winter long. Give them many buckets of water before freeze-up. (See page 149 for a list of frost dates in various cities.)

HOW TO WATER

At first, use a simple moisture metre to calculate how long it takes for water to reach deeply into the soil. It has been estimated that 1 inch (2.5 centimetres) of water will keep your soil moist from 5 to 15 days depending on your soil and the weather conditions. To achieve this same result takes 1 gallon (4 litres) of water per minute per 1,000 square feet (93 square metre) applied for approximately 10 to 11 hours.

SPRINKLER SYSTEM: If you use any of the twirling or revolving, looping back-and-forth systems, set out containers at different parts of the cycle to see how long it takes each to fill with 1 inch (2.5 centimetres) of water.

DRIP IRRIGATION: The most efficient water systems are drip. Hoses set on or in the soil water the roots rather than the surface. It's an abiding regret of mine that I didn't install a drip system when I redid my garden but someday when I tear it all apart, I'll make sure that this is the first thing I invest in. If you are starting a new garden, it is a good idea to figure out right from the beginning which way you'll be watering.

A simple method is to use an ordinary hose from the faucet to the edge of a drip system of feeder lines each irrigating about a 2-foot wide (60-centimetre) swath. You'll need them closer in sandy soil.

CUSTOM WATERING: I usually water my plants by hand. I know this sounds as if I haven't got anything else to do with my time, but I water as soon as the sun comes up—slowly, gently. It's a splendid way to start the day. I can also do a little slug slaughtering at the same time. For special plants I use a dipper, for the rest a hand-held hose with various nozzle selections:

misting, for newly planted seeds; a fine spray for seedlings; a slightly heavy but soft rain-quality spray for transplants. I have indicator plants spread around the garden. When one of them starts to look pathetic, I give it and the surrounding plants a good soak. Otherwise I leave them alone and hope that mulch and the weather will keep things cool and moist. I always have pails of water sitting around to get warm. Not all plants like cold water, certainly the little ones don't. I'm not much on cold showers so I assume plants aren't that crazy about them either. And there are a lot of plants, such as gentians, that can't cope with all the chemicals we have in city water. Let the water sit for twenty minutes so that at least some of these chemicals, such as chlorine, will evaporate.

When to water: Please, please don't water at night. It invites all sorts of bugs into that dampness and encourages mildew. Don't get confused between watering with a sprinkler and the quality of rain at night. The latter is more relentless, and bugs will be scurrying around to get away from it. Besides, there's nothing you can do about it.

Remember that when you use an oscillating sprinkler, you'll lose at least 50 percent, though probably it will be closer to 80 percent, of the water to evaporation and wind. This increases the later in the day you water, depending on how hot it is. Studies at American universities show that the optimum time to water is 5 a.m. If you can't make it out of bed that early, you can get inexpensive handy timers that attach to your water outlet to do it for you. The drawback is that they'll water whether it's needed or not.

If you decide to go with a custom-built automatic watering system, make sure the installer knows something about your watering needs. Be careful to avoid rain shadows (spots where nothing hits) and don't have it timed on an automatic 15 minutes-a-day setting. That's useless—your plants will develop very shallow roots. Timers should be set so that they water for several hours only a couple of times a week. Try to learn how to control the system yourself, so you can shut it off if there's been enough rain. There is nothing quite as discouraging as watching sprinkler systems come on during a downpour.

CONTAINER GARDENING: The beautiful clay and terra cotta pots that look so good in the garden have one major drawback— they lose a lot of water. You will have to water at least once, if not twice, a day. Plastic ones hold water much more efficiently, and the designs have been improved dramatically. If you add a handful of coir to the bottom of the pot, then mix another in the top bit, this will help hold moisture in the soil. But use the old knuckle test: plunge your finger into the pot and if the soil is dry at your second knuckle, water until the water comes right out of the bottom of the pot.

PLANTING

Going to the nursery and buying plants is one of the great pleasures of life. But you've got to be careful here. Many growers use a lot of chemicals such as growth hormones to develop bushy plants. It's usually not necessary; you can find nurseries that grow their own plants and don't depend on chemicals to have saleable plants. One of my nursery heroes is Larry Davidson of Lost Horizons in Acton, Ontario. He was the person who alerted me to this practice many years ago. Now I'm very careful about who I buy from. There are great nursery people all over the world. They will share their accumulated wisdom and help you make good plant choices for your site. If not, move on to someone who will.

Make sure you plant early enough and deeply enough so

that new plants get a chance to establish a good root system before the onset of hot weather. I no longer add any soil amendments or fertilizers to the hole I dig for any given plant. Instead, I use lots of compost or manure around new plants. The nutrients will be absorbed when they're needed, and this method will also protect the soil. Plant late in the afternoon and give them a good soak—never do this in the heat of midday. Try to give new plants a bit of shade for a week or so.

In very dry regions, add water-retentive materials such as coir products. Coir is a renewable resource and so far there have been no reported bad side effects.

PERENNIALS:

- The rule-of-thumb is that they'll need 1 inch (2.5 centimetres) of water a week. Mulch will help the soil retain moisture.
- Some perennials that don't need a lot of water include fescues, junipers (the ground-hugging type), coreopsis, asters and yarrows. Chances are that many of the plants native to your area will also be adapted to drought.

ANNUALS:

- Annuals have shallower roots than most perennials and therefore tend to require more water.
- Annuals that don't require a lot of water include verbena, portulaca and salvia.

SHRUBS:

- Once a plant is more than two years old, you can hold back on watering unless it's looking poorly or wilted; then give it a good soak which means getting water well below the root system.

TREES:

* Trees require less watering than shrubs. They send roots deep into the earth, drawing up moisture and aspirating it into the atmosphere—a kind of air conditioner. The easiest thing to do is just let water dribble in near the base of the tree. Move the hose around and let it go in each area for hours (you'll have to keep checking). You can get a special attachment for your hose that lets you deep-root water very effectively by driving it into the ground near the roots, where the water will be used to its best advantage.

GREY WATER

Like many things in the horticultural world, the old ways are new again. Using grey water is exactly what my grandmother did when she threw the dishwater into her flower garden. The phosphates, even from low-phosphate soap, help plants grow lush foliage. Most flowers like it but acid-loving plants such as rhododendrons and azalea hate it. Be judicious. Studies in British Columbia have shown that plants watered with waste water yielded higher vegetable crops—I can't attest to this, however, since I can't grow vegetables in my shady garden.

But check your local laws, especially if you decide to follow this practice at the cottage. Make sure you aren't aiming at a well. And if you are thinking of directing your automatic dish-washer residue into the garden, you'll have to refit the pipes. This may sound far-fetched at the moment, but suppose severe water rationing comes into effect? Hmmm?

I came across a whole community of gardeners on Toronto Island, each of whom had a form of cistern placed under the downspout from their roofs. It looked like something straight out of my prairie past. In those days no one, but no one, would have allowed a drop of rain to escape. A water butt or cistern is the easiest way to get water with little trouble. One inventive container was an abandoned electric soup tureen from a restaurant. It was large enough and had a spout for pouring off water and a hinged double top.

LAWNS

Lawns are in this section because water is what lawns need most, even when they are established. I'm not a fan of grass and haven't been since I started gardening seriously in the 1980s. It's a difficult ground cover and I'm not wild about mowing. It's become very clear that we have to make lawns much smaller, one element in a garden design rather than the main feature. Use a small bit of lawn as emphasis in your design—background for a woodland or meadow.

If you still have grass, you've got to get it off chemicals if you have been using them. Any kind of artificial fertilizer will kill off the worm population, and worms are crucial to the health of your lawn. Worse: if you've been using chemicals on your lawn, it will need, no, demand larger and larger quantities, like all drug addicts. And your lawn will be much more likely to get a wider spectrum of disease and succumb to drought. Many municipalities now have bylaws restricting chemicals for cosmetic use on lawns. Check out your area's website to see what is and is not allowed if you still feel you must use herbicides and pesticides.

If you use a lawn service, don't let them apply chemicals and fertilizers automatically. Query them and make sure you have a choice. Lawns really don't need that much fertilizing in the first place and you're better off with an organic conditioner for the soil. Your lawn probably needs a fairly neutral soil (a pH of 6.5 to 7.5). Test it with some litmus paper after a heavy rain.

PROPER MOWING:

- No mower does a better job than a regular push mower (a reel mower). Especially good are the ones with self-sharpening blades. A reel mower cuts the grass rather than pulling or taking swipes at it as the rotary ones do. It will even do a better job than an electric mower. Always set the blades so they don't take off more than one quarter of the height of the grass; 2 to 3 inches (5 to 8 centimetres) is a good height. This may mean more frequent mowing but you probably need the exercise anyway. The taller the grass, the denser the canopy. This will also kill off any low-growing weeds. Mow in the evening when the grass is dry. If the grass is wet you may just be spreading diseases around.

- Leave any clippings *in situ*—50 percent of the nitrogen will return to the soil. They will decompose faster than you expect and, since weeds need sun to germinate, it will help keep them at bay. But if you're using chemicals, sweep up clippings and pitch them out in the garbage (not the composter). I once heard a nurseryman on a phone-in radio show say that it was just fine to put grass clippings that had been sprayed with 2,4-D into the composter because it breaks down so quickly. Wrong, wrong, wrong. In all sorts of tests, it's been found that even after a year of hot-rot composting, 2,4-D is still evident. Don't use 2,4-D, but if you already have, don't put grass clippings covered with it in the composter unless it's very late in the season and you've only used it at the beginning of the season.

PROPER WATERING:

- Always water early in the day—the earlier the better.
- Water when the soil has become completely dry, probably

not even once a week, to a depth of of 1 inch (2.5 centimetres) at least. If you have a good water supply, water to
4 inches (10 centimetres).

- Light soils will drain more readily, so they will need more
water. Heavy clay soils, on the other hand, will require
less water.
- Don't water during a drought. Grass will go into dor-
mancy when stressed by drought and will come back
once it has sufficient water. Consistent light watering will
only encourage shallow roots that won't withstand any
further dry conditions. The deeper the roots of your lawn,
the healthier and tougher they'll be.

LAWN PESTS:

- The bug mostly likely to irritate your lawn is the chinch
bug. To find out whether or not you have chinch bugs,
cut both ends off a can, put it into the lawn and fill with
water. If you see chinch bugs floating up, you've got a
problem. Sabadilla dust or *Beauveria bassiana* are natural
ways to control them.
- Diatomaceous earth will control billbugs, nematodes and
most other nasty bits of business.
- *Bacillus popilliae* will control Japanese beetle.

LAWN WEEDS:

- If you are plagued with weeds, increase fertilizing.
- Allow the soil to dry out between waterings to inhibit
weeds from germinating.
- Dig weeds out by hand and be sure to get all the root
system.
- Chunks of yellow or dying bits of grass should be cut
right out and the hole reseeded or sodded.

GREEN TIPS
FEEDING THE LAWN

- Feed your lawn twice a year: spring and fall.
- Top dress with compost in early fall. Mix in grass seed for an extra thick cover.
- Use slow-release fertilizer. You don't want fast-release stuff on a shallow-rooted grass such as bluegrass. Thatch is likely to develop; it won't let water penetrate, and the fertilizer (along with the chemicals) will run off or seep into the water table.
- Slow-release fertilizers improve the health of your grass by creating humus. Humus acts as a sponge to hold nitrogen so the roots can utilize it.
- Organic nitrogen is the most important nutrient your grass needs. Slow-releasing, non-burning nitrogen sources include fish meal, blood meal, hoof and horn meal and canola seed meal.
- Lift out a chunk of grass and have a look at the roots. If they look weak, add bonemeal or any product with a high phosphorus content to give them a boost.
- Sources of organic phosphorus include bone meal, super-phosphate (not all organic gardeners approve of this stuff since it requires sulphuric acid to convert phosphate rock into a product for plants).
- If your grass looks diseased, it probably needs potassium. Try wood ashes.
- Sources of organic potassium include kelp meal, liquid seaweed and wood ashes (from the fireplace not the barbecue).
- Other natural amendments include calcium phosphate, sulphate of potash and sulphate of potash magnesia.
- Sheep manure, bone meal (the coarse form is slower

acting) and cottonseed meal are good organic fertilizers.
* If grass looks on the yellow side, try adding blood meal, manure or cottonseed meal.

LAWN CARE:

* Aerate in spring and fall by walking across the lawn in crampons or golf shoes—actually, there are spikes you can slip on over shoes that do the trick. This will also eliminate thatch—a layer of dead stems and roots that won't let anything penetrate.
* Make pH adjustments in spring: use dolomitic lime to increase alkalinity.
* If you have thatch, aerate the lawn and add some compost. There are heavy thatch rakes designed especially for this problem.
* If you are seeding grass, use a mixture of seeds so that if one variety gets hit with a disease, the others can carry on. Use only hardy grasses.
* If you must use insecticides, look for ones that kill specific insects.
* Pyrethrum-based pesticides (derived from the seed of chrysanthemum) are considered safe but they have recently been found to be dangerous for humans in the misting form. Use only as a last resort and under perfect conditions.
* Don't get sucked in by the generic label "natural" on herbicides or pesticides. Read what the active ingredients are. Terms such as natural, organic and sustainable are thrown about much too casually. Some products once considered safe (for example, glyphosate, which is sold as Roundup) we now know will build up in the water table. Unless you've got a huge infestation of weeds, try everything else first.

* Dispose of any left-over chemicals through your municipality's hazardous waste collection. Buy only as much as you need at any time, and, I repeat, use them only as a last resort.

GROUND COVER ALTERNATIVES TO THE LAWN

There is an ancient rule about the soil: keep it covered because if you don't, the weeds will. Though grass has been regarded as the *ne plus ultra* of ground covers, it isn't really. It doesn't provide habitat for insects, so think about other forms of ground cover. Green isn't the only beautiful colour that nature has supplied us with. Look for the gold, tan and russets of native ornamental grasses, for instance.

Along with providing habitat, ground covers help protect the soil, hold back erosion and provide great beauty. Don't think that a ground cover has to be a very low plant. They can go as high as a couple of feet (60 centimetres). You can be as unconventional as you want. Perhaps you'd like to see a whole lot of one of my favourites: leadwort (*Ceratostigma plumbaginoides*). It has three seasons of colour: green-grey leaves in spring, stunning blue flowers that go on for weeks in late summer and scarlet leaves in fall. It divides easily for spreading around substantial areas.

For damp places, mosses are hard to start but superb once they are established. Try bog rosemary for a slightly acid, damp soil. For shade, consider epimediums, wild ginger, bugleweed, periwinkle, *Astilbe chinensis* 'var *pumila*' and deadnettle (especially *Lamium maculatum* 'White Nancy'). One of my all-time favourite plants is lady's mantle, which does as well in sun as it does in shade—it's so versatile I use it as an edging plant wherever I can. But never let it go to seed or you'll have it everywhere.

Primroses all like rich soil with some shade. Any of the lungworts are also good ground covers (particularly *Pulmonaria* 'Sissinghurst White'). Foamflower (*Tiarella*) is a sea of white flowers in the spring, plus it has the added advantage of attractive foliage.

For sunny places, try woolly thyme (this one loves the warmth of rocks), pussytoes (*Antennaria dioica* 'Rubra') or chamomile. Creeping Jenny (*Lysimachia nummularia*) is a very pretty but invasive plant with brilliant yellow flowers in spring; the cultivar 'Aurea' is slower spreading and I love it. Another beauty is Irish moss (*Arenaria verna* 'Aurea'). Any of the low-growing sedums make splendid ground covers and most are very hardy, sweet William (*Dianthus barbatus*), maiden pink (*Dianthus deltoides*), wild sweet William (*Phlox maculata*), moss-pink (*P. subulata*) and creeping phlox (*P. stolonifera*) all have an honoured place in my garden.

DESIGNER LAWN ALTERNATIVES:

- A lawn of white or Dutch clover can be an excellent cover. White clover draws nitrogen from air into the soil and will improve it immeasurably.
- Sweet woodruff spreads like mad and will grow in fairly deep shade. It has pretty white flowers in spring.
- For a hot, sunny spot, use sedums and hens-and-chicks, which have fleshy leaves and are drought tolerant after they've taken hold. The colours have a wide range, from brilliant red to almost purple. Back them up with 3/4-inch (2-centimetre) gravel for a crisp look. Good drainage is essential.
- Thyme takes a couple of years to turn into a tapestry, but is pure pleasure as an alternative to lawn. Plant about 2 inches (5 centimetres) apart and make sure it's got six

143

hours of sun a day. Water generously for the first few months. Of course, you can't do this if you've got acres to cover up.

- Consider having a flowering lawn instead of a grass monoculture. Use something like English daisy (*Bellis perennis*) or blue-eyed grass (*Sisyrinchium*) or any little flowering spreader native to your area. This needs mowing, but only occasionally—usually at the end of June before dandelions and other sun-loving weeds get a head start. Set your blades about 3 inches (7.5 centimetres) high. In spring, mow around the nicest clumps until plants go dormant.
- There is a relatively new product called Eco-Lawn. It's a mix of organically grown grass seeds that don't require chemical fertilizers and pesticides. It seldom needs watering and grows slowly, so you'll be mowing rarely. It looks lovely.
- For dry shade, try epimediums, hardy geraniums (make a mixture of sizes and colours—-it might be tricky but it will be gorgeous), bellflower (there are lots of little ones that will spread quite nicely); bugleweed (the cultivar *Ajuga* 'Chocolate Chip'has deep purple-black foliage and blue flowers) and deadnettle. Lungworts add a silvery touch.

Spring:
- Winter aconite, snowdrops and hepatica all bloom very early in spring. For hepatica, new leaf growth shows up after it blooms.
- Dutchman's breeches spreads rapidly in a woodland garden. It has ferny foliage and tiny white flowers with yellow tips; plants go dormant in summer.
- Grape hyacinth and daffodils, especially the smaller species, look charming when planted in a lawn.

- Plants that like shade and woodland conditions (soil high in humus, cool) include spring beauty, violets, rue anemone, wood anemone and bloodroot. Trout lily—a subtle beauty with an orchid-like flower—spreads by root shoots and grows into a dense patch. There are three wild gingers (*Asarum*) to choose from: one native to the east, one native to the west and the European kind, which is smaller and shinier than the other two. Virginia bluebells, trillium, wild blue phlox, Labrador violet (an enchanting little violet) and the ubiquitous Johnny-jump-up, which will naturalize everywhere, especially in slightly acidic soil.

Summer:
- Blue-eyed grass has a tiny blue flower in June.
- Deptford pink (*Dianthus armeria*) blooms into September; wild geranium grows in open woods or sunny roadsides but tends to be patchy; butterfly milkweed attracts butterflies and can easily be controlled by mowing.
- Spiderwort likes rich soil and good sun and moves very quickly into any open spot.
- Evening primrose grows in dry sites and grows to 2 feet (60 centimetres). Be careful with this one; it will go everywhere.
- Yarrow provides summer colour. Let a clump bloom, then cut back.
- Heal-all (*Prunella vulgaris*) has purple flowers and tolerates shade.

Fall:
- Wintergreen is evergreen and has scarlet berries in autumn. Asters bloom through the fall, as do black-eyed Susans and goldenrod, a terrific plant that does not cause hayfever.

- Look at roadsides to see what grows best there. Identify plants using a good weed book and try out a section of your garden in this style (for more ideas, see Chapter 10).

XERISCAPING: TWENTY-FIRST CENTURY GARDENING

Xeriscaping is a gardening concept that's been around since the early 1980s and has now become the norm. It works on the principle of low-water landscaping.

GREEN TIPS
THE BASICS OF XERISCAPING

- Use drought-tolerant plants, or plants that have adapted to drier conditions and are reliably hardy in your area.
- Use plants indigenous to a region since they will withstand enormous weather swings much better than more fragile imported plants. They will be less likely to suffer from insect damage or disease.
- Put the right plant in the correct microclimate for it to flourish—that is, don't force a sun-lover into the shade, and vice versa.
- Reuse grey water from your sink or washing machine; use rain barrels; or channel water from the edge of your property to planted areas.
- Use an efficient irrigation system (watering with a hose is always a good one).

Start by making a water plan for your garden. You must think carefully about this concept; we will all be on water metres soon. Do you have areas subject to erosion? Boggy spots? Poor soil? Prevailing winds? A zone map will give you the hardiness zone you live in (examples in the chart at the end of this chapter show when frost comes in and out of some communities). Make yourself sensitive to the various micro-climates in your garden. These will be influenced by the wind patterns, the quality of shade, the amount of sun and reflective light and the proximity to fences, tall buildings and any mature trees.

WATER ZONES: Divide the garden into water zones first, and then decide what to plant where.

- Perennials and small shrubs need a high water zone.
- Lawn areas should be in a moderate water zone.
- Trees and large shrubs require the least amount of water so should be in a low water zone

Make a list of all the plants you have or would like to have, and group them according to their water needs. This may mean moving a lot of plants around but in the long run you will be doing yourself and the garden a favour. And it will mean that you are using whatever water is available most efficiently.

Consider your plants' root systems; how taller plants shade smaller ones; how the trees and shrubs are affecting the air quality. If you take all this into account, you'll be much, much more aware of your plants' water needs.

The water zones also depend on the height of the land, the proximity to a water source, how far your hose system goes, the depth of humus in the soil, and the general quality of the soil you already possess. Use at least 4 inches (10 centimetres) of amendments such as manure and leaf mould. And, of course, mulch (see Chapter 3).

LOW WATER ZONE: Use plants with low water demands. They are very forgiving when a drought comes along. Use these plants in the most exposed spots farthest away from the house.

HIGH WATER ZONE: Put plants that demand the most water and attention within easy reach of the house and a water source.

GREEN TIPS
WATERING WISELY

- Plant so that tall plants will be on the north side of your design, and short plants on the sunnier south side.
- Remember that plants need lots of water when first planted. If they are watered properly, they will get along pretty well on their own after that.
- Use certain plants in separate parts of the garden as indicators—don't water until you see them wilt a little.
- Dig wider holes for your plants at about the same depth as the root system; water the hole if the soil is very dry at the bottom or if you want to check drainage. Don't amend the soil. Amending just pampers them and they go into shock when they move out of this area.
- Humus is necessary; it acts like a sponge, absorbing and distributing water evenly and efficiently to plant roots. A mix of manure and compost will create good organic humus but just settle it around plants rather than mix it into the soil.
- Since many new garden sites are low in organic matter, reserve precious compost for distribution around individual planting holes.
- Keep your garden well weeded because weeds use up a lot of water.
- Keep plants de-stressed by pruning minimally and only for the sake of plant health.
- Use rain barrels at the end of eavestroughs to capture water; or redirect downspouts into the garden.
- When you do need to water, make sure you water deeply.

No sprinkling about of this precious commodity.

- Make sure you have good drainage since most drought-tolerant plants need it. If the soil doesn't drain properly, add lots of organic matter.
- Water only in the early morning or late afternoon. Use a drip system. And if you have a watering system, make sure it's used efficiently. Twenty minutes a day is a waste of water.
- Use a stone mulch: surround plants with 3/4-inch (2-centimetre) gravel, which will let water through and prevent weeds from growing. It also retains heat and supplies minerals.

WATER GUZZLING PLANTS:

- Perennials: bleeding heart, columbines, delphinium, foxglove.
- Lawn: Kentucky bluegrass. Actually, most lawns need way too much water, so consider making lawn areas smaller as the years go by.
- Ground covers: bugleweed, baby's tears, myrtle, pachysandra.
- Shrubs: azaleas, rhododendrons, yew, Japanese snowball tree, red-twig dogwood.
- Trees: weeping willow, magnolia, trembling aspen, flowering dogwood, red and sugar maples.

Whatever you do, don't put in a water-hungry garden. These are referred to by environmentalists as hydroscapes. If everyone practised xeriscaping, water demand could drop by about half. Keep this in mind: "As the greenhouse effect increases, we will see hydrological extremes," says James Hansen, Director of NASA's Godard Institute for Space Studies. "Some areas, especially mid-Continental regions, will have more frequent and extreme drought. At the other end of the spectrum, some areas will have extreme rainfall." Protecting our water is a responsibility for everyone.

FROST CHART:
APPROXIMATE FROST-FREE PERIODS IN SOME
SELECTED AREAS

AREA	ZONE	FROST OUT	FROST IN
British Columbia			
B.C. North	2-7	4 June	3 September
Vancouver Island	8	19 April	5 November
Alberta			
Calgary	3	23 May	15 September
Edmonton	3	7 May	23 September
Saskatchewan			
Regina	2	21 May	10 September
Manitoba			
Thompson	2	15 June	16 August
Winnipeg	3	25 May	21 September
Ontario			
Toronto	6	9 May	6 October
Quebec			
Montreal	5	3 May	7 October
Quebec City	4	13 May	29 September
New Brunswick			
Fredericton	5	18 May	26 September
Nova Scotia			
Halifax	6	6 May	20 October
Prince Edward Island			
Charlottetown	5	17 May	4 October
Newfoundland			
St. John's	5	18 May	4 October

Yukon			
Dawson City	2	13 June	17 August
Northwest Territories			
Yellowknife	2	27 May	15 September

Courtesy of Environment Canada

9

OLD WIVES' LORE

THE GETTING OF WISDOM

If you've ever observed a squirrel with a particularly bushy tail in late September and thought, "It's going to be a cold winter," well, you've been participating in an old wives' tale. This is ancient lore based on observation and passed down through generations almost without examination. Most old wives' wisdom does have some factual basis. In the example of the squirrel's tail, what probably happened is that there was a cool summer; since that's usually followed by a cold winter, the squirrel would naturally have a fuller coat.

Take planting by the moon: transplant on or during a waxing moon. This is an old wives' tale that has real depth. The moon, as we know, has a profound effect on the earth's magnetic field and that in turn modifies growth. It also influences the migration of water moving inside the smallest organism (much like it affects tides). Check this one out yourself—it's more likely to rain after a full or new moon. And this is precisely the weather you want after transplanting.

There is another bit of lore that advises you to plant in the buff. Since I do most of my gardening wearing not very much at all, I'd attest to that. But what the folklorists probably had in mind was that it should be warm enough so you could plant while naked. Plants are responsive to the smallest energy fluctuations.

In the 18th century, people believed that you should never plant the same thing in the same place twice. We call this crop rotation and, of course, it is the most sensible way to keep from depleting the soil. Except we now know that you shouldn't plant members of the same family in the same place twice.

In earlier times, people had a more harmonious coexistence with nature. The game to be eaten was first praised, the peach or pear replanted. Nature was not "red in tooth and claw" but the great instructor. Nature was to be observed, to be learned from. In the ecological garden, we return to some of these practices. You can take this ancient wisdom with a grain of salt or you can fall in with old patterns of observing the moon's cycles while making your garden plans.

All this was very apparent to Rudolf Steiner back in the 1920s when he developed a theory of planting called biodynamic agriculture. While investigating crop failures he had been asked to examine, he pointed out that the decline in nutrient content of soil was due to the introduction of synthetic fertilizers and chemical pesticides. This in turn introduced crop diseases and insect pests. He developed a philosophy that all organic matter should be returned to the soil using compost, nitrogen-fixing plants, and companion planting. This is what we would now call sustainable farming or gardening. But his ideas were more controversial. He was convinced that the lunar phases were key to the growth of plants and that they dictated the optimal times to plant or transplant and when growth would be stimulated. I've seen biodynamic farms and tasted wine from a biodynamic winery in Italy, and they are magnificent.

Alan Chadwick brought Steiner's ideas to North America in the 1960s, leading to the California movement of using local products to develop their special cuisine. Chadwick, too, believed in intensive planting and companion planting, as well as in making compost from medicinal plants such as yarrow, chamomile, stinging nettle, oak bark, dandelion and valerian. This idea makes a lot of sense; they add essential nutrients such as sulphur, potash, nitrogen, calcium, silica and phosphoros.

To be a close observer of nature, start with the phases of the moon:

First quarter: Lunar gravity draws water through soil causing seeds to swell and burst, ergo good germination. Sow annuals such as lettuce, cabbage, spinach, broccoli, cauliflower, corn and grains.

Second quarter: Moonlight is stronger and gravitational pull less intense, which leads to strong leaf growth. Sow beans, tomatoes, melons, squash and peppers.

Third quarter: Moonlight diminishes after the full moon. Plant root crops: potatoes, beets, carrots and onions. Plant evergreens and bulbs.

Fourth quarter: There's even less gravitational pull and moonlight. Till the soil, prune shrubs and trees, and kill weeds. Mow the lawn.

GREEN TIPS
FACTS ABOUT THE SUN AND MOON:

• The new moon waxes, or increases, until it becomes full, then it wanes or decreases.

- The moon aligns itself with the sun twice a month, as well as with Saturn.
- The sun travels through the entire zodiac, spending one month in each constellation. The moon spends three days in each constellation.
- Precipitation falls within three days of the new moon, so they say. It is usually dry at the midpoint of the waxing or waning moon.
- The moon is farther from the sun in summer and winter. At its perigee (nearest point) to the earth, plants will be vulnerable to pests and fungal diseases.
- An ascending moon fills plants with vitality.
- A descending moon will favour roots (good time for trans- planting).
- When the horns of the crescent moon are sharply defined, there will be high winds. When they are dull, it will be humid.
- In fall, when the face of the moon is very sharp, expect frost.
- Since sap flow slows down during the ascending moon, this is a good time to prune.
- When the moon is low on the horizon, in autumn and winter, concentrate on composting, cutting, rooting and adding food to the soil.
- Harvest during a full moon for the best-looking fruits and vegetables.
- A new moon will mean ants and sea animals are listless—watch what they are doing.
- Thunder as the moon changes means the weather will be moist.
- Pollinating insects have energy and vigour at night with the waxing moon, and are too tired to go about their

business during the day.
- Pollinating insects have most energy during the day when the moon is in its first quarter.
- The nearer the moon's change is to midnight, the fairer the weather will be for the next seven days.
- The nearer the moon's change is to noon, the more foul the weather for the next week.
- Full moon at the equinox means violent storms followed by a dry spring.

PLANTING CYCLES

Once you've got decent soil—even in just some parts of your garden—there are important decisions to be made about planting. Watch for the signs that tell you when is the best time. Here are some of the signs that guided the ancients:
- Plant annuals in increasing light: new moon to full moon.
- Plant biennials, perennials, bulbs and root plants in decreasing light: full moon to new moon.
- Never plant on Sunday—this day is ruled by the sun and is considered dry and barren.
- Don't plant on the first day of the new moon, or on days the moon changes quarters.
- The last quarter of the moon is the best time for preparing soil for cultivation.

February:

Aquarius—January 20 to February 19
- Airy, dry tendencies; barren and masculine characteristics.
- According to Indian legend, the position of the moon during the first two weeks of February indicates whether

the growing season will be wet or dry. If the horns of the moon point down, the moon is emptying its water—be ready for a wet spring and summer.

- A dry moon with horns pointing up means you should plant early and use drought-resistant seeds.
- A new moon in Aquarius is a prediction that the crop will be poor because of blight or insects.
- If there was a full moon from the 1st to the 19th of February, it was believed that the following summer's gardens would thrive.
- In February or March while the moon is passing through the moist sign of Pisces, cuttings should be planted in cold frames in rooting sand when moon is in first quarter.

March:

Pisces—February 19 to March 21

- Under the fruitful sign of Pisces, the moon's path is positioned above the plane of the earth's orbit. When this happens, it's good for planting (not in all parts of our country, of course). Pisces holds water and has feminine, productive characteristics.
- Start seeds in a cold frame. It's a sign for strong roots.
- Plants shoot up if seeded after March 21.
- First and second quarters of the moon are increasing phases—plants that produce yield above ground should be planted.
- The third quarter is a decreasing phase. Root crops—carrots or turnips, for instance—should be planted during this period.
- In the fourth quarter, pull weeds, cultivate and turn sod.

April:

Aries—March 22 to April 20

- Fiery, dry, windy and barren characteristics; not the best planting time, especially in the fourth quarter.
- Dig the soil and destroy noxious weeds. Turn sod and start to plant especially during the last quarter of the moon or first three days of a new moon.
- In the first quarter, plant broccoli, barley, cabbage, corn, lettuce, chard, kale, endive, oats, rye, spinach and leafy vegetables.
- In the second quarter, plant beans, peas, squash and tomatoes.
- In the third quarter, plant beets, carrots, parsnips, potatoes, radishes, rutabagas, turnips, onions and bulbous flowering plants.
- The fourth quarter is bad for seeding. Prepare the soil instead.

May:

Taurus—April 20 to May 21

- Earthy, moist; a good time to plant since this is a productive sign. Seeds will have great vigour at this time.
- Avoid the first day of the new moon for planting; wait to plant leafy vegetables in the waxing moon.
- In the second quarter, replant snap beans and summer squash.
- Fertilize or side dress with compost or mulch.
- Cultivate during the fourth quarter of the moon.

June:

Gemini—May 21 to June 20

- A sign of aridity and barrenness; destroy weeds, trim, cut timber, build fence posts and cultivate the soil.

Cancer—June 21 to July 22

- Pregnant moon in June means enough rain to support a late crop.
- This is one of the most productive times for planting. You'll get a good crop and have a chance of plants maturing under Cancer.
- This is the time to finish planting the main garden.

July:

Cancer—June 21 to July 22

- This is a fruitful, watery, feminine sign.
- Fertilization of cucumber flowers by insects is said to be affected by the moon: When it's a new sliver, the bugs rest at night and are vigorous by day.

August:

Leo—July 22 to August 23

- This is a lofty, firm, steadfast sign. Leo's characteristic are fiery, dry, barren and masculine.
- Crops harvested under the influence of Leo will keep better for a longer time.

September:

Virgo—August 23 to September 23

- An earthy dry sign; harvest root crops during the waning moon.

Libra—September 23 to October 23

- Moist semi-fruitful characteristics with airy masculine tendencies; harvest in the third or fourth quarter.

October:

Libra—September 23 to October 23

- This is a moist sign so harvest crops during the waning third or fourth quarter.
- If you plant during the water sign of Pisces, it's logical that you harvest during the sign of Libra, which is also a water sign and completes the cycle.

November:

Scorpio—October 23 to November 22

- This is a watery, fruitful, feminine sign.
- It's the best time to harvest apples and mulch herbs.
- Propagate hardwoods during the waxing moon. Take hardwood cuttings from all kinds of deciduous trees and shrubs as well as evergreens, yews, boxwood and hollies. Slips should be tied into bundles and kept in damp sand in a cool dark place.

December, January:

Sagittarius—November 22 to December 22

- This is a masculine sign, fiery, dry and barren.

Capricorn—December 22 to January 20

- Radically prune grapes during the second quarter of Capricorn—if pruned on the swelling moon, grapes will grow round and juicy.

WEATHER

An important aspect of ecological gardening is being in tune with the universe. You become a weather watcher, sensitive to changes in the moon, cloud formations and the direction of the wind. Weather affects all our senses dramatically. Gardeners are subconsciously aware of this, but it is satisfying to be a little better informed. The ancient wisdom and lore have a lot to tell us. A few weather facts:

- Rain and lightning are fertilizing agents. When lightning strikes, the high temperature in the vicinity of the lightning bolt causes oxygen and nitrogen in the air to react, forming nitric oxide. With rain, it becomes nitric acid, a nutrient plants can use.
- Sulphur comes with rain.
- Snow has nitrogen, phosphorus and other minerals (really helps the crops in the north).
- Fog contains iodine, nitrogen and chlorine.
- Dust restores minerals to exhausted soil and contains bacteria.
- An attractor of static electricity (a metal pole) will increase the size of tomato plants.
- From 3 a.m. until noon, sap rises. From 3 p.m. until midnight, the lower parts of plants are influenced by the revolution of the earth. Therefore, harvest leafy vegetables in the morning and root crops in the afternoon.
- Falling barometric pressure, which precedes a storm, means that the atmospheric pressure on your body falls, less oxygen is rushing around in your body and you feel sluggish.
- Good weather means high barometric pressure, therefore less humidity, more energy and better feeling all around.

SOME ANCIENT WEATHER PROPHECIES:

- Dew needs a clear sky and a windless night. A cloud cover holds heat and won't allow the drop in temperature required for condensation. When night breezes move warm air over the ground, they prevent the formation of dew. Morning dew embodies the conditions for fair weather.
- Fog forms on windless, cloudless nights. But in winter, it is the result of warmer, wet air blown over cold land surfaces.
- Winter: *Clear moon/ Frost soon.*
- Night-time weather: *Cold is the night/ When stars shine bright.*
- Foul weather: When there's a large halo around the moon, there will be heavy rains soon.
- Smoke that goes to ground rather than rising indicates that there's a storm brewing—the air pressure is dropping.

GREEN TIPS
OBSERVATIONS FROM OLD WIVES AND HUSBANDS

- Sow early peas for rabbits, broadcast lettuce to fool the birds, and plant cabbage to satisfy early butterflies.
- If you grow hens-and chicks (*Sempervivum*) on your roof, you will keep lightning from striking it. And witches will avoid your house.
- Transplant when leaves of the sugar maple, lilac and cottonwood flip over to show their light undersides.
- When barn swallows are really striking out for mosquitoes, it means that their wings are weighted down in heavy air. The soil will be moist.
- In the East, cabbage flies finish laying eggs when the dogwood trees bloom; wait to set out brassicas and they

won't be bothered by root maggots.

- Chard and beets planted after the lilacs have bloomed won't be bothered by leafminers.
- When waterfowl seem to be flying high, it means the air pressure is lowering and bothering their sensitive ears.
- Increased air pressure is likely to make animals restless.
- When a storm is coming, sap rushes to plants' roots to prepare them for the onslaught. It rushes back to the branches and leaves to repair any damage when the storm is over.
- Chickweed, dandelion and daisies close up when air pressure drops.

Though we can all learn from the sayings of the past, of course, being gardeners, we apply common sense to what we do, and work with what the garden provides.

10

STYLES OF GARDENING

Agarden overloaded with exotics, straining against its sur-
roundings, is not only poor design, but also less likely to
survive in these days of climate change. The great landscape
designers of our time are looking toward ornamental grasses
rather than lawns; they no longer sneer at native plants as
being too coarse or vulgar. And they've stopped imitating
English and European formal designs. Gardening in North
America has come into its own.

Any kind gardening, from vegetable to herb to perennial,
is a form of partnership with nature. If you adjust your style
to the kind of soil and weather conditions of your region, you
will be able to practise effective gardening. Thus, you avoid
the nonsense you see in Southern California—desert country
but people insist on green, green grass, swimming pools, foun-
tains and lush plants. They have changed the water table, but
even this hasn't yet discouraged them from wasting water.
With this change, there are more drying winds and many more

terrifying wildfires. One of the saddest photographs I've seen is the one of a Los Angeleno spray-painting the dead stuff outside his house a vivid green.

Imagine, for instance, that these people were living *with* the land instead of on top of it. They'd be developing beautiful desert and drought-resistant gardens that would fit into the landscape and add to its biodiversity. Gardening isn't a form of wish-fulfilment or self-indulgence. It is about enhancing where you find yourselves gardening. Our responsibility as gardeners is to leave things better than we find them, not change things to our own whims.

THE NATURAL GARDEN

Don't clunk meadow in-a-can seeds all over the front garden. You might, if the bed is prepared carefully, get a rather glorious show the first year. But the next year, only the strongest will survive. And each year—unless you tend it carefully—you'll end up with a field of one aggressive plant. Probably goldenrod.

A natural garden takes careful thought. You must be familiar with plant communities: what lives well with what. It can take many forms: woodland, meadow or prairie. It's a contained wilderness, if that isn't too much of a contradiction in terms. Once a natural garden is mature, it will probably require much less maintenance than a conventional garden.

A natural garden doesn't have to have only native plants. What you want is any kind of plant that has adapted to your terrain and to the amount of water you can afford to give it. For instance, hybrid tea roses are tricky creatures, fussy and demanding, but rugosa and shrub roses are tough and very hardy. Switch. Don't look for sexy or trendy hybrids, look for the simplest forms. Anything that is closest to the species is the one for you.

Natural design takes just as much careful thought as any other. Choose a balanced mix of flowers, grasses, even weeds. Don't chop everything down but leave plants with dramatic seedheads so you—and the birds—can enjoy them all through the winter. Use the understory of trees and shrubs for woodland plants, thus echoing the wild. Nature is the inspiration you turn to for planning as well as for the plants you choose.

Ideally, you'll want something that captures the essence of a natural plant community. You don't really want a meadow in the back forty, nor a complete prairie habitat in a small front garden. What you want is the feel of it, an aspect of its soul.

What you also don't want is some big useless landscape that doesn't fulfil any function except to look green. Which it won't, if we go through increasing dry periods as greenhouse-effect experts warn us.

GREEN TIPS
CREATING THE NATURAL GARDEN

- If you must have lawn, choose grasses that are extremely hardy to your area; consider switching to Eco-Lawn.
- If you're using non-native plants, find plants that have adapted well to your climate.
- Learn which native plants thrive best and introduce them to your landscape. Use non-indigenous plants if they are well adapted to climate conditions similar to your own.
- Try to use plants that have more than one function. For instance, any plants in the pea family fix nitrogen in the soil; many edible herbs provide both subtle beauty and a haven for bees; perhaps a beautiful ground cover will also be excellent for stopping erosion.

- Choose a wide variety of plant families so you won't be wiped out if a disease happens to come your way.
- If you look to hybrids, make sure they've been improved in the right way—not for double blooms, frills and freakish size, but for hardiness, drought resistance and scent.

Plants in the following lists are suggestions only, because each region across the country differs and suitable plants will depend on your hardiness zone, the altitude you live at, prevailing winds and availability of water.

GARDENING WHERE IT'S DRY

A really dry garden will have poor soil, probably quite sandy, and you will have to build it up with as much organic matter as possible. The soil will drain very swiftly. Therefore, this is the situation where you hit the street and gather up everyone else's unwanted leaves.

THE DRY GARDEN:

- Think of the silver plants—most of them like sun and have adapted very well to little water.
- Succulents, such as sedums and hens-and-chicks, conserve water in their thick fleshy leaves.
- Shrubs and ground covers that tolerate drought include semi-arid shrubs, aspen, ninebark, buffaloberry, sweet mock-orange, mahonia and potentilla.
- Good grasses for dry conditions include crested wheatgrass, buffalo grass and Canada bluegrass.
- Ground covers for the dry garden include penstemon, woolly thyme, blue veronica, Greek yarrow, hardy pink, and rock soapwort.
- Try perennials such as santolina, basket-of-gold, creeping

phlox, white yarrow, ox-eye daisies, coneflowers, penstemon, Iceland poppy, gaillardia, yucca, evening primrose, prickly pear cactus and many different forms of epimedium.

- Herbs that prefer dry conditions include creeping, woolly and lemon thyme, golden marjoram, oregano, lavender, santolina, yarrow, sage, creeping mahonia and chamomile.

Surely this is one type of garden where the lawn is totally out of place. Look away from the lush greens to tawny tones, subtle colours and lots of movement. I love Mediterranean plants in the dry areas of the garden including as many different kinds of lavender as I can collect. They come up at different times and a couple keep flowering right to the end of October. If you are in a zone that's warm enough, try rosemary—in my Zone 6 garden, different varieties of rosemary plants in big terra cotta pots maintain a touch of the exotic and provide glorious scent. It does mean that they have to be brought in during the winter. If I lived in a warmer zone, I'd grow citrus plants, lily-of-the-Nile and, certainly, bougainvillea.

THE DESERT GARDEN: Keep an eye out for plants suited to the hottest, driest places. Again, think first of the silver foliage plants. Sagebrush has beautiful leaves in summer but they are dry in winter; prickly pear cactus, hawthorn and silver-leafed buffaloberry are good choices.

Keep an eye out for red spider mites. Mottling of leaves will be an indication. Spray plants with water and try to make a direct hit on any webs that develop.

When planting, add a fistful of oats or barley to ferment and produce heat for the newly forming roots.

Succulents (echeveria, aloe, agave, sedum and euphorbia), rosemary, thyme, purple alyssum and sea lavender are all good accent plants in the desert garden.

PRAIRIE GARDEN: The prairie garden is a dry meadow garden. Use herbaceous rather than woody plants. These are plants that die back to the soil and go dormant only to reappear the following spring, thus avoiding the ravages of winter winds. They need at least six hours of sunshine. To ensure that you have the right mix, you will be better off if you remove your lawn or present garden a bit at a time and plant islands of plants. As usual, make it a mixture of annuals and perennials. Any prairie garden should include some grasses and a combination of flowers.

Flowering time for most prairie plants is summer and early autumn rather than spring; remember this when you are choosing your plants.

* Flowers for a dry prairie garden could include sea holly, purple coneflower, asters (there are dozens native to each part of the country), purple flowering gayfeather, prairie coneflower, compass plant, big or little bluestem grass, false indigo and prairie coreopsis.

A MEADOW GARDEN: You can't go wrong with black-eyed Susan, butterfly weed, wild ginger, crested iris, sweet cicely, bee balm, California poppy.

OASIS PLANTING: Plan a dry garden around one area and direct water to that area to create an oasis of edible plants. Feed and care for the oasis separately from the other. For the oasis, you'll need mulch and rich soil. The edibles require water (the true cottage gardens of old had the vegetable and cutting gardens close to the house, where water was available, and the ornamentals farther away).

For the edibles in your oasis, use nut and fruit trees, fig, grape, Jerusalem artichoke (well contained or they'll go everywhere), mulberry, olive, persimmon, and herbs such as thyme, oregano, rosemary and marjoram.

GARDENING WHERE IT'S WET

WETLAND GARDEN: If you have wetlands instead of a formal water garden, why not let it be as natural as possible—perhaps extend a well-designed platform or bridge into it. Alas, what you don't plant here any more is the flashy and gorgeous purple loosestrife. It's just too dangerous in boggy or wet ground because it will take over. Even the hybrids must be avoided.

Plants for a wetland garden include ferns, hostas, rodgersia, iris, cattails, lotus and water lilies, buttonbush and red osier dogwood.

SEASIDE GARDEN: Grasses and sedges do very well in wet soil; they include silver feather grass, papyrus, feather reed grass, maiden grasses including zebra grass, drooping sedge, Gray's sedge, corkscrew rush, Japanese sweet flag, manna grass and silver spike grass. For a ground cover, rugosa rose will tolerate salt spray very well.

WOODLAND GARDEN: Natives for a moist woodland garden include rue anemone, trillium, trout lily, spring beauty and toothwort. Check out the list of native plants for more suggestions (see page 179).

JAPANESE GARDEN: If you decide to try to create a Japanese garden (ideal for moderate sites that aren't too dry or too wet), please, please, don't think that putting in a few rocks, raking some gravel flat and adding a couple of plants alongside a Japanese statue or lantern is going to make such a garden. The Japanese have a long, exceedingly complicated history bound up in their gardens and the placement of every rock is significant. One of the easiest, most foolproof things to start with is a dry stream bed—collect smooth stones and arrange them like a little river in the garden so they are either a feature or the focus of your design. The essence of the Japanese garden is simplicity and elegance—no clutter, a place for contemplation. Dwarf evergreens look appropriate in this setting. If you are interested in bonsai, you now have a place for these dwarf plants. Try the following: Japanese black pine, azalea, creeping lilyturf (good for both sun and shade), camellia, black mondo grass, blue fescue, moss sandwort, heavenly bamboo and yew. In colder regions, lily-of-the-Nile in large pots looks stunning; in warmer areas, grow directly in the garden.

GARDENING WHERE IT'S COLD

The northern garden has special qualities. Long, long summer days for quick growing compensate for protracted winters. Look for plants that are listed in seed and nursery catalogues as being completely hardy. Lots of hardy shrubs will survive being killed right down to the ground and come back again in the spring.

- Be sure to water all evergreens heavily before the onslaught of the first freeze-up. If trees and shrubs have to go through a winter without heavy-duty watering before hard frost, they are likely to be affected by sun and wind damage.
- Northern gardens usually have a deep and consistent snow cover to help them through the winter. But make sure branches aren't overloaded with snow and ice, and that ice hasn't accumulated at the base of plants.
- Plan the garden around the colour of trees and shrubs when they are not in bloom, since winter hangs on for such a long time.

• Ground covers for the northern garden include Arctic phlox, sweet autumn clematis, kinnikinnick, snow-in-summer, sedums and Virginia creeper.

SELF-SOWING GARDEN

One of the easiest gardens, certainly one that will sit lightly on the land, is a self-sowing garden. It's almost impossible to imitate perfect informal drifts. Move any volunteer seedlings around once you learn how to identify them and stick them in the right place. I like to leave a couple of places in the garden where nature can take its own course, and usually it looks marvellous.

Be sure to deadhead all summer long and then let selected plants go completely brown and dry. The wind, birds and your movement in the garden will sow the seed. Shake the seeds where you want them. Mark where these plants are or you'll dig them up in the spring. On the other hand, they may surprise you and that's always a welcome quality in the garden. Just don't let strong volunteers crowd out or starve weaker plants.

Encourage growth among paving stones and stone walls if you're lucky enough to have either. All around walls in the Mediterranean, you'll find red valerian. It has enchanted me since the first time I saw it. Keep on deadheading and it'll carry on blooming (leave a few seedheads, though, if you want it to self-sow).

One of my favourite self-seeders is one I brought back from Salt Spring Island many years ago. It's rose campion. It's a terrific plant with wonderful grey foliage and brilliant magenta flowers that keeps on blooming practically to death—good cutting plant, too. If you find the colour too strong, keep the flowers cut so that you can appreciate the extravagant silver foliage.

My neighbour Amanda has forget-me-nots all over her garden and now they're in mine. Wallflowers, snapdragons, mulleins and foxgloves are all enthusiastic self-seeders.

One of my all-time heroes, the late British gardener extraordinaire Christopher Lloyd, recommended Mexican fleabane or daisy and spurge.

Remember that hybrids won't come true from seed. That means you won't get exactly what you planted the first time and the results might be dreary, but sometimes they can be quite fascinating. I have some candytuft that self-seeds and each year it changes colour: now it's heading for whites and pinks instead of the original lilac.

One columbine that I let go to seed has turned around several times, has become smaller and sometimes has more interesting colours. I deadhead anything dull, then take the ones I particularly like and isolate them just to see what will come up next year.

Fall planting of self-seeders: You can plant the following seeds in fall and not worry about them. I could never remember where I'd put things, but eventually I got smart—now I mark the areas. Sow in fall just the way you would in spring, or let the flowers themselves set seed (just don't deadhead or pick them all): amaranth, California poppy, China asters, cleome, corn cockle, cornflower, cosmos, datura, delphinium, forget-me-not, Chinese forget-me-not, gaillardia, hollyhock, love-in-a-mist, mignonette, nicotiana, pinks, annual poppies, portulaca, sage, painted-tongue, silene, snapdragons, snow-on-the-mountain, stock and sunflowers.

ANNUALS	Height	Colour
California Poppy	12"-24" (30cm-60cm)	yellow to orange
Candytuft	16" (40cm)	many colours
Cornflower	12"-48" (30cm-120cm)	white, pink, blue
Cosmos	36"-72" (90cm-180cm)	white, pink, red
Forget-me-not	12"-24" (30cm-60cm)	blue
Love-in-the-mist	18"-24" (45cm-60cm)	blue,white
Marigolds	4"-24" (10cm-60cm)	yellow, red
Nasturtium	7"-24" (18cm-60cm)	yellow to orange to red
Pot marigold	12"-24"- (30cm-60cm)	yellow to orange
Statice	24" (60cm)	yellow, lavender
Sweet alyssum	3"-12" (8cm-30cm)	white to violet
Zinnia	12"-30" (30cm-75cm)	many colours

PERENNIALS	Height	Hardi-ness Zone	Month of Bloom	Colour
Candytuft, Iberis semperviens	12" (30cm)	3	April-May	white
English daisy, Bellis perennis	6" (15cm)	3	April-June	white, pink, purple
Feverfew, Chrysanthemum parthenium	12"-36" (30cm-90cm)	4	July-August	white
Foxglove, Digitalis	36" (90cm)	4	June-July	white to purple
Golden margerite, Anthemis tinctoria	36" (90cm)	3	July-August	yellow

Lupine	30"-60"		June	many
Lupinus	(30cm-			colours
	150cm)	3-6		
Mountain bluet,	24"		June-	red
Centaurea	(60cm)		August	
montana		2-3		
Sweet violets,	8"		April, May	violet to
Viola odorata	(20cm)	6		white

BIENNIALS

Dame's rocket	36"-48"		July-	white,
Hesperis	(90cm		August	purple
matronalis	120cm)	2-3		
Hollyhock	9'		July-	many
Alcea rosea	(270cm)	2-3	September	colours
Honesty	36"		July-	white,
Lunaria annua	(90cm)	8	September	purple
Moth mullein	36"-48"		June-	white and
Verbascum	(90cm-		September	pink
blattaria	(120cm)	3		
Evening primrose,	36"-48"		July-	yellow
Oenothera	(90cm-		September	
biennis	120cm)	4		
Sundrops	24"-36"		July-	yellow
O. fruticosa	(60cm-90cm)	4	September	

Edible herbs also work beautifully in the self-sowing garden—or arrange them in pots throughout if you don't want them to spread. Annual herbs include borage, chervil, dill, marjoram and summer savoury. Perennial herbs include catnip, chamomile, hyssop, salad burnet and tansy.

ENDANGERED BULBS

Bulbs make wonderful garden additions. They aren't only for spring; there are also superb bulbs for the summer garden. But serious problems have emerged. Some bulbs have been collected in the wild in such profligate amounts for so many decades that they're now on the endangered species list. If you are fond of the following bulbs, please purchase them from reputable sources such as seed exchanges. Hold off buying them from nurseries—that is, until you can be assured that they have actually been cultivated under nursery conditions. Apparently, many of them are collected in the wild, then repackaged as a nursery-grown product. Look for symbols that indicate they are not wild collected. Many of the more responsible nurseries are waiting until there is nursery-grown stock to sell to their customers. It's better to go that route.

Always check where these bulbs are from when you buy them: *Anemone blanda, Arisaema, Cardiocrinum giganteum, Cyclamen* (but not *C. persicum*), *Cypripedium, Dracunculus vulgaris, Eranthis cilicica, E. hyemalis, Galanthus* (but not *G. nivalis*), *Iris acutiloba, I. sibirica* ssp. *elegantissima, I. paradoxa, I. persica, I. tuberosa, Leucojum aestivum, L. vernum, Narcissus asturiensis, N. bulbocodium* var. *conspicuus, N. bulbocodium* var. *tenuifolius, N. cyclamineus, N. juncifolius, N. rupicola, N. scaberulus, N. triandrus* 'Albus', *N. triandrus* var. *concolor, Pancratium maritimum, Sternbergia* spp., *Trillium* spp., *Urginea maritima, Uvularia.*

PLANTING BY INDICATORS

Indicator plants are those plants that give you information about the conditions in your garden. I have a couple of indicator plants in each part of my garden. If they flop about looking wilted, I water. I don't bother if they seem to be able to take it. There are lots of ways to use indicators and I've tried to mention them in each chapter where it's relevant.

But there is a larger issue here. Some plants are also recognized as "biological measuring sticks" of their habitat. This is called phenology. These plants reflect changes in their environment such as seasonal temperature increases. The following list includes some of the plants used on Plant Watches; they are chosen as indicator species that bloom in response to rising temperatures. They are tracked all over the country and you can sign up to be a tracker. (For more information, visit http://www.naturewatch.ca/english/plantwatch/dandelion/glossary.html.)

Populus tremuloides Trembling aspen:
YK, NT, BC, AB, SK, MB, ON, QC, NB, NS, PEI, NL
Arctostaphylos uva-ursi Bearberry:
YK, NT, NU, BC, AB, SK, MB, ON, QC, NB, NS, PEI
Galium boreale Northern bedstraw:
AB
Clintonia borealis Bluebead lily:
ON, QC, NB, NS, PEI, NL
Houstonia caerulea Bluets:
NS
Cornus canadensis Bunchberry:
YK, NT, BC, AB, SK, MB, ON, QC, NB, NS, PEI, NL
Ranunculus glaberrimus Sagebrush buttercup:
BC
Prunus virginiana Chokecherry:
AB
Rubus chamaemorus Cloudberry:
YK, NT, NU, MB
Tussilago farfara Coltsfoot:
NS, NL

Vaccinium vitis-idaea Lowbush cranberry:
YK, NT, NU, MB

Taraxacum officinale Dandelion:
YK, NT, BC, AB, SK, MB, ON, QC, NB, NS, PEI, NL

Ledum groenlandicum Labrador tea:
YK, NT, NU, BC, AB, SK, MB, ON, QC, NB, NS, PEI, NL

Larix laricina Larch:
YK, NT, BC, AB, SK, MB, ON, QC, NB, NS, PEI, NL

Syringa vulgaris Common lilac:
YK, NT, BC, AB, SK, MB, ON, QC, NB, NS, PEI, NL

Pinus contorta Lodgepole pine:
BC, AB

Lupinus arcticus Arctic lupine:
YK

Acer rubrum Red maple:
SK, MB, ON, QC, NB, NS, PEI, NL

Epigaea repens Trailing arbutus:
NS

Dryas integrifolia / D. octopetala Mountain avens / white
  mountain avens:
YK, NT, NU, BC, AB, MB, ON, QC

Anemone patens Prairie crocus:
YK, NT, AB, SK, MB

Clintonia uniflora Queen's cup:
BC

Rhododendron canadense Rhodora:
NB, NS, PEI, NL

Amelanchier spp. Serviceberry:
YK, NT, BC, AB, SK, MB, QC

Saxifraga tricuspidata Three-toothed saxifrage:
YK, NT, NU, MB

Saxifraga oppositifolia Purple saxifrage:
YK, NT, NU, BC, AB, MB, ON, QC

Maianthemum stellatum (formerly *Smilacina stellata*) False
  Solomon's seal:
AB

Trientalis borealis Starflower:
NB, NS, PEI, NL

Fragaria virginiana Virginia strawberry:
YK, NT, BC, AB, SK, MB, ON, QC, NB, NS, PEI, NL

Myrica gale Sweet gale:
NL

Trillium grandiflorum Large-flowered trillium:
ON, QC

Linnaea borealis Twinflower:
BC, AB

Nymphaea odorata Fragrant water lily:
ON, QC

Elaeagnus commutata Wolf willow:
AB

NATIVE PLANTS FOR THE GARDEN

Here is a list of garden-worthy native plants divided into gen-
eralized regions for Canada and the northern United States. You
must never rip native plants out of the wilderness unless the
land is threatened or it's your own property. It's better to buy
these plants from local nurseries where they guarantee that the
plants have been propagated specially for the garden. Find a
trustworthy nursery where they understand the nature of native
plants and know how to fit them into the ecological garden.

Plant some or all of these natives for each season. When
you are planting them, make sure you prepare the soil properly. Woodland plants require lots of humus (compost), but

most prairie and meadow plants do well in nutrient-poor soil. They should be watered deeply for the first few months and then left to nature's devices.

Point to remember: Evergreens will not only be interesting in winter, but also provide nesting areas. Plants marked with an E are ephemerals. They bloom in very early spring when native insects such as bumblebees are looking for something to eat. So it's important to have them in the garden. Those marked D are drought tolerant, and HR means heat resistant.

EASTERN FOREST (northern hardwood forest):

American beech	*Fagus grandifolia*
American chestnut	*Castanea dentata*
American cranberry	*Vaccinium macrocarpon*
American hazelnut	*Corylus americana*
American wild plum	*Prunus americana*
Basswood	*Tilia americana*
Black locust	*Robinia pseudoacacia*
Carolina silver bell	*Halesia carolina*
Cherry birch	*Betula lenta*
Dwarf huckleberry	*Gaylussacia dumosa*
Eastern cottonwood	*Populus deltoides*
Eastern hemlock	*Tsuga canadensis*
Eastern hop hornbeam	*Ostrya virginiana*
Eastern red cedar (D)	*Juniperus virginiana*
Eastern redbud	*Cercis canadensis*
Eastern white pine	*Pinus strobus*
Flowering dogwood	*Cornus florida*
Highbush blueberry	*Vaccinium corymbosum*
Kentucky coffeetree (D)	*Gymnocladus dioicus*
Ohio buckeye	*Aesculus glabra*

Pignut hickory	*Carya glabra*
Pinxter flower	*Rhododendron periclymenoides*
Pitch pine	*Pinus rigida*
Red maple (HR)	*Acer rubrum*
Red oak	*Quercus rubra*
Rosebay rhododendron	*Rhododendron maximum*
Sassafras	*Sassafras albidum*
Shagbark hickory	*Carya ovata*
Silver maple	*Acer saccharinum*
Spicebush	*Lindera benzoin*
Striped maple	*Acer pensylvanicum*
Sugar maple	*Acer saccharum*
Sumac (D)	*Rhus* spp.
Tulip tree	*Liriodendron tulipifera*
Viburnum (HR)	*Viburnum* spp.
Virginia pine	*Pinus virginiana*
White elm	*Ulmus americana*
White oak (D)	*Quercus alba*
Yellow birch	*Betula alleghaniensis*
Witch-hazel	*Hamamelis virginiana*

EASTERN FOREST UNDERSTORY:

American ginseng	*Panax quinquefolius*
Bellwort	*Uvularia grandiflora*
Bloodroot	*Sanguinaria canadensis*
Blue cohosh	*Caulophyllum thalictroides*
Bluebead lily	*Clintonia borealis*
Cardinal flower	*Lobelia cardinalis*
Evening primrose (D)	*Oenothera biennis*
Indian hemp	*Apocynum cannabinum*
Jack-in-the-pulpit	*Arisaema triphyllum*
Large-flowered trillium	*Trillium grandiflorum*
Mayapple	*Podophyllum peltatum*

New England aster	*Symphyotrichum novae-angliae*
Ohio spiderwort	*Tradescantia ohiensis*
Pokeweed	*Phytolacca americana*
Round-lobed hepatica	*Hepatica americana*
Showy lady's-slipper	*Cypripedium reginae*
Solomon's seal	*Polygonatum biflorum*
Spotted jewelweed	*Impatiens capensis*
Spring beauty	*Claytonia virginica*
Squirrel corn	*Dicentra canadensis*
Sweet cicely	*Osmorhiza longistylis*
Trailing arbutus	*Epigaea repens*
Trout lily	*Erythronium americanum*
Violet	*Viola* spp.
Virginia creeper	*Parthenocissus quinquefolia*
Virginia waterleaf	*Hydrophyllum virginianum*
White baneberry	*Actaea pachypoda*
Wild columbine	*Aquilegia canadensis*
Wild ginger	*Asarum canadense*
Wild potato vine	*Ipomoea pandurata*
Wild sarsaparilla	*Aralia nudicaulis*
Wintergreen	*Gaultheria procumbens*
Yellow lady's-slipper	*Cypripedium pubescens*
Wood sorrel	*Oxalis montana*

BOREAL FOREST:

Balsam fir	*Abies balsamea*
Buffaloberry	*Shepherdia canadensis*
Crowberry	*Empetrum nigrum*
Fireweed	*Epilobilum angustifolium*
Jack pine	*Pinus banksiana*
Labrador tea	*Ledum groenlandicum*
Paper birch	*Betula papyrifera*
Pin cherry	*Prunus pensylvanica*

Sedge	*Carex* spp.
Tamarack	*Larix laricina*
Trembling aspen	*Populus tremuloides*
White spruce	*Picea glauca*

PRAIRIE GRASSES:

Big bluestem (D)	*Andropogon gerardii*
Buffalo grass (D)	*Buchloe dactyloides*
Indian grass (D)	*Sorghastrum nutans*
June grass (D)	*Koeleria macrantha*
Little bluestem (D)	*Schizachyrium scoparium*
Prairie cord grass	*Spartina pectinata*
Prairie dropseed (D)	*Sporobolus heterolepis*
Sideoats grama (D)	*Bouteloua curtipendula*
Switchgrass (D)	*Panicum virgatum*

PRAIRIE FLOWERS:

Bergamot (D)	*Mondarda fistulosa*
Black-eyed Susan (D)	*Rudbeckia hirta*
Blue false indigo (D)	*Baptisia australis*
Butterfly milkweed (D)	*Asclepias tuberosa*
Compass plant (D)	*Silphium laciniatum*
Culver's root (D)	*Veronicastrum virginicum*
Cup plant (D)	*Silphium perfoliatum*
Goldenrod (D)	*Solidago* spp.
Ground-plum vetch (D)	*Astragalus crassicarpus*
Ironweed (D)	*Vernonia fasciculata*
Leadplant (D)	*Amorpha canescens*
Pale purple coneflower (D)	*Echinacea pallida*
Prairie blazing star (D)	*Liatris pycnostachya*
Prairie crocus	*Anemone patens*
Prairie rose (D)	*Rosa acicularis*
Prairie smoke (D)	*Geum triflorum*
Purple prairie clover (D)	*Dalea purpurea*

Rattlesnake master (D)	*Eryngium yuccifolium*
Spotted Joe-Pye weed	*Eupatorium maculatum*
Wild blue lupine (D)	*Lupinus perennis*
Yellow prairie coneflower (D)	*Ratibida columnifera*

PACIFIC NORTHWEST:

Arbutus	*Arbutus menziesii*
Big-leaf maple	*Acer macrophyllum*
Camas	*Camassia quamash*
Cascara	*Rhamnus purshiana*
Devil's club	*Oplopanax horridus*
Douglas fir	*Pseudotsuga menziesii*
	syn. *P. taxifolia*
Fairy slipper	*Calypso bulbosa*
Inside-out flower	*Vancouveria hexandra*
Nootka false cypress	*Chamaecyparis nootkatensis*
Ocean spray	*Holodiscus discolor*
Oregon grape	*Mahonia aquifolium*
Pacific dogwood	*Cornus nuttallii*
Pacific rhododendron	*Rhododendron macrophyllum*
Pacific yew	*Taxus brevifolia*
Red alder	*Alnus rubra*
Red elderberry	*Sambucus racemosa*
Red huckleberry	*Vaccinium parvifolium*
Salal	*Gaultheria shallon*
Salmonberry	*Rubus spectabilis*
Sitka spruce	*Picea sitchensis*
Skunk cabbage	*Lysichiton americanum*
Sword fern	*Polystichum munitum*
Western bleeding heart	*Dicentra formosa*
Western hemlock	*Tsuga heterophylla*
Western red cedar	*Thuja plicata*

NATIVE PLANTS WE LOVE TO HATE:

Horsetail joint grass	*Equisetum* spp.
Jerusalem artichoke	*Helianthus tuberosus*
Poison ivy	*Toxicodendron radicans*
Stinging nettle	*Urtica dioica*
Vine maple	*Acer circinatum*
Wild sweetpea	*Hedysarum mackenzii*

11

FINALE

W e can all crumple under the weight of the sad news about our home and planet, or we can try to make a difference. There have been so many improvements since the 1990s, it's sometimes good to catalogue them: we have hundreds more organic farms and their attendant farmers' markets; restaurants specialize in organic food; we can buy paint that doesn't contain toxins; and many of the industrial chemicals that have kept us from being healthy are now outlawed.

Nurseries are likely to have ghastly chemicals under lock and key (it's where they make hefty profits, which is why they still sell them). And many nurseries are using Integrated Pest Management in their growing practices—developing future plants with the environment in mind.

Even though the news isn't perfect, don't listen to people who think it's pointless to try to live a sensible, sustainable life. They use China and India as an excuse to carry on as though the planet won't run out of resources, including such basics as water and air. They are wrong; we all have to work to improve things.

If we had all picked up the message in 1991, we'd have produced a couple of generations of kids and politicians by now who'd assume that most of the suggestions in this book were second nature. Well, don't let another decade go by without making changes in your own life and in your gardening. These small changes will add up, and the more you do to make your own footprint smaller, the more you will expect both governments and businesses to do the same.

Here are Bridget Stutchbury's suggestions for what we can do in our everyday lives. Her book *Silence of the Songbirds* is must reading.

- Buy shade-grown coffee, which increases tropical forest habitat for birds; also look for fair-trade and organic coffee, which will put fewer pesticides into the environment.
- Choose organic produce from South America; this will reduce the amount of dangerous pesticides used, kill fewer birds and be safer for farmers and consumers.
- Buy organic North American produce: ditto above.
- Buy wood and paper products certified by the Forest Stewardship Council; this will increase the amount of forest being logged sustainably.
- Buy recycled paper products (toilet paper, paper towels), unbleached by chlorine, to reduce logging pressure on forests and increase habitat for birds.
- Turn off lights at night in city buildings during birds' peak migration period.
- Keep your cat indoors; fewer birds will be killed and your pets will be healthier.

GREEN TIPS

MAKE A POLLINATOR-FRIENDLY GARDEN

One out of every three mouthfuls of food we eat is dependent on the free service provided by a pollinator. Dr. Laurence Packer, a.k.a. the Bee Guy, of York University recommends the following:

- Design the garden so there is always a succession of plants in bloom from spring through fall.
- Use plants native to your region that provide nectar, pollen and/or act as host plants for butterflies, bees and other insects.
- Provide nesting sites such as dry stems, wood blocks drilled with variously sized holes for twig-nesting bees or a sunny patch of bare ground for ground-nesting bees.
- Avoid pesticides.
- Supply water for all wildlife. A suspended milk carton with a pinhole in the bottom works well, but avoid standing water, which provides breeding habitat for mosquitoes.

(Source: *A Guide to Toronto's Pollinators*, published by the David Suzuki Foundation.)

HOW TO MAKE THE GARDENERS OF THE FUTURE: Help out with a local school program or community gardening allotment program. Get kids interested. They pick up so many messages from us; if we're terrified of bees, so are they. Here are a few suggestions for your children:

- Make a patch of garden that is strictly theirs and keep out. This can be a shady part for a fort (nothing fancy—old boxes will do); or a vegetable garden. Just as long as it's a secret place and very personal. A space in a shrub can become a secret hut—a weeping shrub will do.
- Most kids love digging—let them help. They'll discover

that worms aren't yucky in the hand, that lots of bugs are not scary but fascinating. Teach them which are friends.
- Show them how to live with insects but make some rules. For instance, never swat at a bee when it's feeding on nectar; don't touch certain plants that might be poisonous; don't let them pick up any bug they don't recognize. But whatever you do, don't overload children with too many rules—it will ruin the pleasure of the garden.

If they make mistakes and you lose a few plants, it isn't a disaster. Include children in the gardening chores that are most fun:
- Watering with a nice long wand and gentle spray.
- Planting seeds that are guaranteed to have spectacular results: scarlet runner beans, pumpkins, sunflowers. If they can end up eating whatever they plant, it's even more successful. It will also make the connection between the soil and their food, something they won't get in a supermarket.
- Placing stones for a pathway. They will place them at the distance they need to hop about.
- Cleaning up interesting tools.
- Helping to cut plants back.
- Making a mulch mix of leaf mould, coir and compost, manure; or helping brew some manure tea.
- Allowing them to get dirty.

Animals are rather more truculent. The only thing that keeps cats out of borders is to put in little pointed sticks around vulnerable plants. As far as dogs go, you have to leave a spot for them to be on their own. You can set up minimal barriers and hope that, by planting as intensively as possible you will discourage them from running about the garden; dogs are trainable, unlike most of their owners.

By not making the garden too sacrosanct a place, by giving it the feeling of an extension to the house, by making it useful as well as beautiful, the garden can become a valuable teaching tool as well as a sanctuary.

HOW TO SOLVE THE CHRISTMAS TREE PROBLEM: Here's the dilemma—you don't really want to buy a plastic creation but can't bear the thought of chopping down another tree. Don't feel guilty. Christmas tree farms breed trees to be harvested. Make sure yours comes from a farm and not from the wild. And after the holidays, recycle your Christmas tree:
- Tie the whole thing, or just branches, to the fence and add bits of popcorn, cookies and fruit for birds.
- Put the branches in window boxes; add dried berries and seed pods.
- Use branch tips for sachets or potpourri; use large branches as mulch.
- Wire wide branches over trellised vines to protect them from drying out.
- Chop large branches into mulch for acid-loving plants.
- Dry the trunk for firewood or garden stakes.

But if this still isn't the route you want to take, buy a small conifer (less than 5 feet/1.5 metres) in a 5-gallon (20-litre) pail. Prune in early fall after shoot growth is over and before new growth starts. Mulch around the tree. Dig a hole where you want to put the tree after Christmas; fill it with leaves. Don't allow the soil you take from the hole to freeze (keep it in the basement). Bring the tree inside as close to Christmas as possible. Make sure it isn't near either heat or light sources. After two weeks—no more—return it to the garden. Moisten the preserved hole with warm water, pop in the tree, add the preserved soil and put leaves around as a mulch.

HOW TO BECOME MORE ENVIRONMENTALLY FRIENDLY AT HOME:

- Recycle all paper; and reuse shopping bags and containers.
- Recycle properly in the blue box, if your community has a curbside recycling program.
- Segregate your garbage into organic matter, packaging, recyclable containers, reusable containers and products.
- Buy in bulk (taking along your own containers). Remove excess packaging at the checkout counter, explaining in a brief and friendly way why you are doing this.
- Compost all organic matter.
- Don't purchase anything that's environmentally unfriendly (for example, carry your own reusable coffee mug with you instead of using a Styrofoam one; don't buy large plastic garbage bags, plastic wrap or baggies).
- Don't use plastic bags for dog poo; instead, get a coffee can, put a used coffee filter in it and put the dog's dropping in this. Then recycle the droppings in a pet composter (see page 31)
- Save the cardboard cylinders from wrapping paper to make collars for young plants to protect them from cutworms.
- Use only recycled paper.
- Switch to environmentally friendly household cleaners which you either purchase or make yourself. They are just as effective as chemicals.
- Use rags instead of paper towels; cloth napkins instead of paper; and toilet tissue and sanitary products made of recycled materials.
- Be aware of the source of the foods you buy and avoid those whose production endangers the environment either through pesticide use or destruction of rainforests for agricultural purposes.

- Buy produce in season as much as possible and try switching to organically grown produce. Balance costs by serving more meatless meals.
- Shop locally.
- Use energy-saving products such as rechargeable batteries and full-spectrum fluorescent bulbs.
- Return to the old days as far as energy use is concerned—turn off lights, etc. When purchasing appliances, consider their energy consumption.
- Use a bike or walk if possible; use public transportation.
- In a barn-burner of a speech in July, 2008, Al Gore said "Enough solar energy falls on the surface of the earth every 40 minutes to meet 100 percent of the entire world's energy needs for a full year." Get behind renewable energy projects such as wind, solar and and geothermal power. Green roofs should be mandatory on all new buildings: they reduce heat, save water and lower the amount of air conditioning needed.
- If you must drive, observe the speed limit—it will reduce your gas consumption by 20 percent; keep your car as light as possible; or get involved with a car-sharing program.

Remember: environmentalism makes sense—it isn't kooky or anti-industry or unrealistic. It recognizes the necessary limits to our planet's resources. It tries to minimize our destructive impact on air, water and the earth-support systems on which all life depends. Environmentalism is everybody's business. Follow the precepts of nature. In her amazing book *Biomimicry,* Janine M. Benyus writes:

Nature runs on sunlight.

Nature uses only the energy it needs.

Nature fits form to function.

Nature recycles everything.
Nature rewards cooperation.
Nature banks on diversity.
Nature demands local expertise.
Nature curbs excesses from within.
Nature taps the powers of limits.

Remember the words of the immortal Pogo: "We have seen the enemy—and it is us."

APPENDIX

ORGANIC AMENDING

MATERIAL (rapid, medium, slow release)	N	P	K
Blood meal (r)	15	1.3	.7
Bone meal (s)	4	21	.2
Cattle manure (m)	2	1.8	2.2
Cottonseed meal (s-m)	7	2.5	1.5
Dried blood (m-r)	12–15	3.	-
Fish emulsion (m-r)	5	2	2
Granite dust (s)	5		
Leaf mould (composted m)	.6	.2	.4
Mushroom compost (m)	.4-.7	57–62	.5–1.5
Oak leaves (r)	8	.4	.2
Phosphate rock (vs	4	2	4
Seaweed (s-m)	1.7	.8	5

SOIL TYPES

	Look	Feel
Clay	Cracked, crusty, shiny, like plastic when wet.	Hard when dry sticky when wet forms large lumps.
Sandy	Loose, porous; won't hold shape.	Easy to work dries fast.
Loam	Full of crumbs, spongy.	Easy to work; well-drained and aerated.

SOIL AMENDING METHODS

Clay	Lots of organic matter.
	Lime to improve texture.
	Green manure.
	Dig up in fall to overwinter.
Sandy	Organic material with coir.
	Compost.
	Leaf mould.
Loam	Keep the nutrient level up with organic material.

BIBLIOGRAPHY

Andrews, Brian. *Northern Gardens*. Edmonton: Lone Pine Publishing, 1987

Appelhof, Mary. *Worms Eat My Garbage*. Kalamazoo, MI: Flower Press, 1982

Ball, Jeff. *Rodale's Garden Problem Solver: Vegetables, Fruits, and Herbs*. Emmaus, Pa.: Rodale Press, 1988

Bartholomew, Mel. *Square Foot Gardening*. Emmaus, Pa.: Rodale Press, 1981

Benyus, Janine M. *Biomimicry: Innovation Inspired by Nature*. New York: Quill, 1997

Boland, Bridget and Maureen Boland. *Complete Old Wives' Lore for Gardeners*. London: Bodley Head, 1976

Bonar, Ann. *The Garden Plant Survival Manual*. London: Quill, 1984

Bremness, Leslie. *The Complete Book of Herbs*. Montreal: Reader's Digest Association, 1989

Buther, Gerald W., Edward Jackson and Richard Sudell.

Simplified Gardening. London: Ernest Benn Limited,

Campbell, Stu. *Let It Rot!: The Gardener's Guide to Composting*. Pownal, Vt: Garden Way Publishing, 1975

Cox, Jeff. "The Pacific Northwest" in *Organic Gardening* (July/August 1990): 26

Druse, Ken. *The Natural Garden*. New York: Clarkson N. Potter, Inc., 1989

Foster, Catharine Osgood. *Organic Flower Gardening*. Emmaus, Pa.: Rodale Press, 1975

Firth, Grace. *A Natural Year*. New York: Simon and Schuster, 1972

Franck, Gertrud. *Companion Planting*. Wellingborough, England: Thorsons Publishing Group, 1983

Galston, Arthur W. *Green Wisdom*. New York: Perigee, 1981

Gershuny, Grace and Joseph Smillie. *The Soul of Soil*. Quebec: Gaia Services, 1986

Hansen, James, "Global Warming Twenty Years Later," ([2008] columbia.edu/ jeh1/2008/TwentyYearsl ater20080623.pdf).

Hansen, James, quoted in "Water Wisdom" by Victoria Mattern in *Organic Gardening* (February 1990): 41

Henderson, Peter. *Practical Floriculture*. New York: Judd Company, 1869

Hill, Stuart B. *Agricultural Chemicals and the Soil*. Paper presented at Chemicals and Agriculture, Problems and Alternatives conference, Fort Qu'Appelle, Saskatchewan, 1977. "The pesticide debate" in *Agrologist*, Vol. 12, no. 1 (1983)

Howard, Robert. *What Makes the Crops Rejoice*. Boston: Little, Brown, 1986

Kruckeberg, Arthur R. *Gardening with Native Plants of the Pacific Northwest*. Vancouver/Toronto: Douglas & McIntyre, 1982

Lee, Albert. *Weather Wisdom*. Chicago: Congdon & Weed, 1976

McHoy, Peter. *Anatomy of a Garden*. London: Marshall Cavendish, 1987

Page, Robin. *Weather Forecasting The Country Way*. Harmondsworth: Penguin, 1987

Riotte, Louise. *Astrological Gardening*. Pownal, Vt: Garden Way Publishing, 1989. *Carrots Love Tomatoes*. Pownal, Vt: Garden Way Publishing, 1975. *Roses Love Garlic*. Pownal, Vt: Garden Way Publishing, 1983

Rubin, Carole. *How to get your lawn & garden off drugs*. Ottawa: Friends of the Earth, 1989

Smith, Miranda and Anna Carr. *Rodale's Garden Insect, Disease & Weed Identification Guide*. Emmaus, Pa.: Rodale Press, 1988

Stutchbury, Bridget. *Silence of the Songbirds*. Toronto: HarperCollins, 2007

Tompkins, Peter and Christopher Bird. *Secrets of the Soil*. New York: Harper & Row, 1989

Encyclopedias:

Harris, Marjorie. *Botanica North America*. New York: HarperCollins, 2005

The Canadian Encyclopedia. Edmonton: Hurtig, 1988

Encyclopedia of Organic Gardening, The. Emmaus, Pa.: Rodale Press, 1978

Encyclopedia of Natural Insect & Disease Control. Emmaus, Pa.: Rodale Press, 1984

INDEX

Page numbers in boldface indicate illustrations